OSPREY AVIATION ELITE • 8

352nd Fighter Group

The FLYING SCOT

SERIES EDITOR: TONY HOLMES

OSPREY AVIATION ELITE • 8

352nd Fighter Group

Thomas G Ivie

OSPREY
PUBLISHING

Front cover
In a major air battle over the oil refineries at Merseburg, in eastern Germany, on 2 November 1944, pilots from the 352nd FG's 328th FS shot down a record tally of 25 enemy fighters. During the engagement, flight leader Capt Donald S Bryan spotted a formation of at least 50 Bf 109s preparing to intercept the bomber stream. Quickly realising that the only way he was going to break up the enemy attack was to lead his flight head-long into the Messerschmitts, Bryan did just that. During the course of the action which ensued, he destroyed five Bf 109s, thus becoming an 'ace in a day'. In Jim Laurier's specially-commissioned cover painting Capt Bryan (in P-51D-10 44-14061 *Little One III*) is seen just seconds after despatching his fifth, and final, victim. His recollection of this final kill was detailed in his combat report;

'I proceeded to attack the lead ship of the enemy aircraft, and got strikes on him. One of my guns stopped firing at this time so I had only one gun firing, and it threw me off a bit. I found it difficult to get many strikes while closing from 350 to 150 yards. When I closed to about 80 yards, I got strikes through the fuselage and wing roots. I broke off the attack and the enemy aircraft went through the undercast at 4000 ft in a very steep dive, indicating about 350 mph, with much black smoke pouring from it. I claim this enemy aircraft destroyed. I then climbed back to altitude and returned to base without further incident.'

The combat report for Capt Bryan's epic sortie is reproduced in full in chapter seven

Dedication

This book is dedicated to my good friend Joseph Howard Longfellow, whose support and assistance during this project was invaluable.

First published in Great Britain in 2002 by Osprey Publishing
Elms Court, Chapel Way, Botley, Oxford, OX2 9LP

ISBN 1 84176 382 9

Edited by Tony Holmes
Page design by Mark Holt
Cover Artwork by Jim Laurier
Aircraft Profiles by Tom Tullis
Origination by Grasmere Digital Imaging, Leeds, UK
Printed through Bookbuilders, Hong Kong

02 03 04 05 06 10 9 8 7 6 5 4 3 2 1

ACKNOWLEDGEMENTS

This book would not have been possible without the generous assistance of many people, and I would like to extend to them my deepest appreciation for their help. Individual assistance came from Charlie Arrington, Donald S Bryan, Bobby Dodd, Carleton Fuhrman, Albert Giesting, Jeff Grosse, Marc Hamel, William N Hess, J Griffin Murphey III, Robert H Powell Jr, Luther Richmond, Alden Rigby, Samuel Sox Jr, Arthur Snyder and James N Wood. I would also like to thank the 352nd FG Association and its members for their continuing support of my efforts in documenting the group's magnificent contribution to victory in World War 2. Finally, I would like to thank my wife Mary for her help and support with this project.

CONTENTS

ACTIVATION AND TRAINING

In September 1942 the American Eighth Air Force, based in England, was still in the process of building up its strength in order to play a major role in the struggle against the powerful German Luftwaffe. At this stage of the war the Luftwaffe was still a formidable foe, and it would have to be eliminated before Allied forces could attempt an invasion of Hitler's 'Fortress Europe'. To accomplish its task VIII Fighter Command needed to create a large force of skilled pilots flying superior aircraft.

While the handful of units sent to VIII Fighter Command in late 1942 carried on the struggle in the European Theatre of Operations (ETO), the USAAF at home was rapidly establishing new fighter groups to augment its forces throughout the world. Such units are not created and trained overnight, however, and nearly two years would pass before the Eighth Air Force received its full complement of 15 groups.

One of the new fighter groups created in the autumn of 1942 was the 352nd FG, which was constituted by a War Department letter dated 29 September, and activated at Bradley Field, Connecticut, 48 hours later. Although no one could have predicted it at the time, the 352nd FG was to become one of the most successful fighter groups in the Eighth Air Force.

The 352nd claimed its first victory on 26 November 1943, and from that point onwards it destroyed German aircraft in record numbers. Indeed, so effective were the group's pilots that when their distinctive blue-nosed Mustangs made their first appearance over Germany, head of the Luftwaffe, *Reichsmarschall* Hermann Göring, reportedly said, 'I knew the war was lost when I saw the "Bluenosed Bastards of Bodney" over Berlin'! By war's end the pilots of the 352nd were officially credited with the destruction of 792.5 aircraft, and this placed the group fourth among Eighth Air Force fighter units.

The 352nd's beginnings were rather inauspicious, for it was a newly created and untested wartime unit with no history or traditions for its leaders to call upon. Two of its assigned squadrons, the 21st and the 34th FSs, had originally been formed during World War 1, but following the armistice they were quickly deactivated. As war clouds began gathering around the world in 1939, the United States started to slowly rebuild its air force, and as part of this expansion these two units were reactivated (as pursuit squadrons) on the same day, 1 February 1940. The third squadron, the 328th, was a newly created unit.

During the first month of its existence the 352nd FG, under the command of Lt Col Edwin M Ramage, was based at Bradley Field, Connecticut. It then moved to Westover Field, Massachusetts, where the group stayed until 15 January 1943. On this date the 352nd returned to Connecticut and settled in at Trumbull Field. Group personnel were less than enthused about their new post, for the base was unfinished and muddy, and the wartime tar-paper buildings were virtually impossible to keep warm. While Headquarters 352nd FG personnel were settling in at Trumbull Field, its assigned squadrons began to arrive at the base.

The first to show up was the 21st FS under the command of Capt William Hennon, a veteran of the bloody fighting in the Philippines and in the defence of Australia. During those dark days from 8 December 1941 through to mid-March 1942, Capt Hennon had destroyed seven Japanese aircraft and became one of the USAAF's early World War 2 aces.

After being reactivated in 1940 and equipped with the Curtiss P-40B, the 21st PS (redesignated a fighter squadron in May 1942) had initially been based in California, before being ordered to Nichols Field, in the Philippines, in November 1941. When the Japanese struck the Philippines on 8 December 1941, Nichols Field was hit hard and the 21st suffered heavy losses in both personnel and aircraft. One of its pilots, Lt Jack Donalson, was able to take off and destroy two of the attacking aircraft.

During the next two months of the Japanese onslaught the 21st was virtually wiped out. Donalson was a lucky survivor, finishing his days in the Philippines as an infantryman, before eventually making it back to the United States and an assignment to the 352nd FG's 34th FS.

Donalson's new unit also arrived at Trumbull Field on 15 January 1943, the 34th FS being led by Capt John C Meyer. He had assumed command of the squadron upon his return from a tour of duty in Iceland.

Like the 21st PS, the 34th PS (also redesignated a fighter squadron in May 1942) had also fought in the Philippines and suffered heavy losses, with the Japanese attack on Clark Field on 8 December 1941 destroying 12 of its 18 obsolete Seversky P-35A fighters and leaving the remaining six damaged. As a result of this raid the squadron did not see action until Christmas Day 1941 when it received some P-40s, which were used by the unit's pilots to claim a few aerial victories before the fall of the Philippines.

Enemy action, accidents and a lack of spare parts quickly reduced the number of Curtiss fighters available to the unit, however, and when none of their aircraft remained airworthy the men of the 34th, like those of the 21st, fought on as infantrymen during the last weeks of the campaign.

Three days after the arrival of the 21st and 34th FSs at Trumbull Field, the 328th FS, under the command of Capt John Poston (also a combat veteran of the defeat in the Philippines), joined the 352nd FG. Training began in earnest.

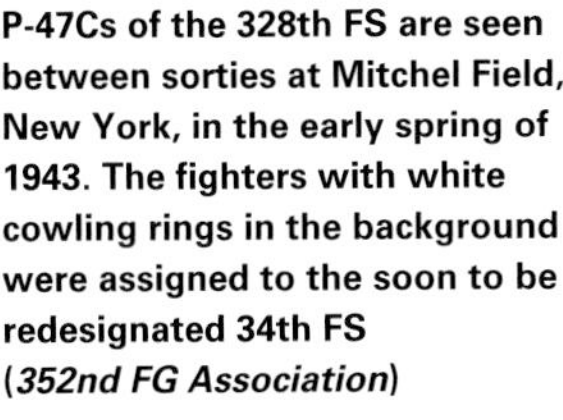

P-47Cs of the 328th FS are seen between sorties at Mitchel Field, New York, in the early spring of 1943. The fighters with white cowling rings in the background were assigned to the soon to be redesignated 34th FS (*352nd FG Association*)

P-47C-1 41-6135 was serving with the 34th FS when it was redesignated the 487th FS at Mitchel Field in May 1943. Few photographs exist of the early Thunderbolts flown by the 352nd FG in the US (*Albert F Giesting*)

The group's P-47s began to arrive on 18 January 1943, and even though the winter weather was often so bad that the training schedule was interrupted for days at a time, the 352nd pressed on. Three weeks later the terrible weather claimed the lives of four pilots from the 21st FS, who had been sent to Providence, Rhode Island, to ferry factory-fresh P-47Cs back to the base. Immediately after they took off on the return trip the weather worsened, reducing visibility to zero-zero, and all four aircraft crashed shortly afterwards.

As training progressed the 352nd FG picked up its first 'operational duty' when, as Ralph Hamilton of the 34th FS put it, the group 'became the defenders of New York City'. The enlarged training programme and the standing alerts prompted moves for all three squadrons. On 17 February 1943 the 328th moved to Mitchel Field, New York, and the 21st FS was sent to Farmingdale, New York. The final move took place on 8 March when the 34th FS joined the 328th at Mitchel Field.

During the following weeks the pilots of the 352nd continued their work of perfecting formation flying, aerial gunnery and strafing, along with undertaking defensive patrols over New York City. Needless to say, these high spirited young fighter pilots periodically threw out the prescribed training schedule and replaced it with one of their own. Larry 'Mac' McCarthy of the 328th recalled;

'One of our favourite activities was bouncing the P-47s of the 21st and 34th FSs during our patrols over New York City. On one occasion when we bounced the 34th FS, a pilot from that squadron momentarily forgot that he was carrying "hot" guns, and nearly shot up one of our Thunderbolts.'

On another occasion a pilot carrying out a practice strafing run on some storage tanks in Brooklyn also forgot about his 'hot' guns and peppered the tanks soundly. The pilots also derived great pleasure from buzzing Yankee Stadium and disrupting the game. McCarthy cautioned though, 'You had to be careful and not make more than one pass over the stadium so as to keep from being reported.'

As the training progressed the pilots began experiencing some problems with their Thunderbolts, and more lives were lost. Both mechanical and operational maladies afflicted the group, with 'gremlins' in the P-47C's exhaust system resulting in a number of fatalities. The 34th FS lost at least one pilot as a result of this problem, Don Dilling remembering;

'We lost Jerry Powell – he just disappeared one day. We sent him off on a high altitude mission and he just didn't come back.'

Dilling nearly lost his life in the same manner. During a training flight he received a radio message directing him to deliver his P-47C to a newly formed unit. Dilling complied with his orders and was returned to his unit by a utility aircraft. Two days later the fighter blew up, killing the pilot. Problems within the exhaust system, and a pre-flight requirement to tighten the carburettor hose clamp before each flight, were the culprits. The continual tightening caused the welds to break and gas spewed into a malfunctioning exhaust system, resulting in an explosion. Once these problems were corrected, training continued without further incident.

Oxygen failure and compressibility added to the list of casualties as training continued. On the plus side, one pilot of the 34th FS survived compressibility in a high-speed dive because of his renowned strength. John Bennett, whose nickname was 'Muscles', pulled his Thunderbolt out of its deadly near vertical descent and brought his heavily damaged fighter back for an uneventful landing. Upon closer examination of the tortured P-47, it was discovered that Bennett had actually bent the control stick by pulling so hard on it as he brought his ship out of the dive! 'Mac' McCarthy recounted;

'Johnny Bennett was an extremely strong physical specimen. He used to win bets in bars doing a one-handed hand press from the vertical to the horizontal position. Nobody believed that it could be done, and in those days few could accomplish it. When John got into a compressibility one day he literally yanked it out of that dive by sheer strength. Believe it or not, he "Class 26ed" that aeroplane pulling out of that dive, bending the stick and doing other damage.'

According to Don Dilling, Bennett had specifically flown this mission after two aircraft had recently been lost due to compressibility dives. As a direct result of these crashes all pilots had been instructed to avoid high speed dives in the P-47. Bennett's response to this order was 'To Hell with this. If I'm going to fly this thing in combat, I want to know what it can do'. So he took his P-47 up and nearly ripped it apart bringing it out of compressibility. That incident may have delayed his promotion to first lieutenant.

Most of the accidents involved the Thunderbolt, but it was a routine training flight that claimed the life of the 21st FS's commanding officer. On 31 March Capt Bill Hennon took off in a BT-14 trainer from Farmingdale and headed for Trumbull. He never arrived. Despite the unit conducting an extensive search of the area, no trace of Capt Hennon, or his aircraft, was found.

2Lt John 'Muscles' Bennett of the 34th FS managed to pull his P-47C out of a compressibility dive and survive. The Thunderbolt did not fare as well, and was withdrawn from use. Also nicknamed 'Tarzan' due to his physical strength, Bennett would enjoy a long association with the 352nd FG, serving with the group from November 1942 through to April 1945, when he left the unit with the rank of major. He completed 134 missions (500 hours) during his time in the ETO, flying both P-47Ds and P-51B/D/Ks with the 487th FS. Bennett also claimed two aircraft destroyed (including a shared kill on the very first mission in which the 352nd FG engaged German fighters) and three damaged in the air, and one destroyed and one damaged on the ground (*Donald K Dilling*)

Maj Luther Richmond assumed command of the 486th FS after the tragic death of Bill Hennon. Seen here at Bodney posing with his personal P-47D-5 42-8412 *"Sweetie"* in early 1944 (he had by then been promoted to lieutenant colonel), Richmond would remain CO of the unit until 15 April 1944, when he was shot down by flak whilst strafing Vechta airfield, south-west of Bremen. Flying his 67th mission at the time, Richmond was at the controls of his new P-51B-10 43-7196 *"Sweetie II"* when the fighter was hit by several well-aimed rounds, leaving its pilot with little choice but to bail out and become a Prisoner of War (PoW). Richmond claimed just one aerial victory – a Bf 109 shot down east of Vechta just minutes before he was himself 'winged' by flak (*Sheldon Berlow*)

April 1943 saw changes in command in two of the squadrons. On the 21st Maj Luther Richmond assumed command of the 21st FS following the loss of Hennon, and a few days later Maj Everett Stewart replaced John Poston as CO of the 328th FS.

More changes took place in May as the 352nd entered its last full month of training, and they were significant changes. The first took place on the 18th when Lt Col Joe L Mason replaced Lt Col Edwin Ramage as commanding officer of the 352nd FG. A few days later two of the group's squadrons were re-designated when the 21st FS became the 486th FS and the 34th became the 487th FS. The latter changes were not well received by the personnel of the 21st FS, as they were quite proud of their unit's combat heritage.

The reason for the re-designation of the 34th FS took on a more humorous note. Rumour had it that the 34th was changed to the 487th as a result of a large number of outstanding debts from the Officers' Club at the old 34th base in the Philippines – debts which no one in the new 34th wanted to pay!

By the last week in May 1943 the 352nd had developed into a well disciplined outfit, and with its training nearing completion, the group was ordered back to Trumbull Field to finalise the programme. Rumours were now rampant that the 352nd was about to be deployed overseas, and the speculation was that they would be going to England.

In June 1943 the rumours became fact as the 352nd FG received its movement orders and began shutting up shop at Westover in preparation for its departure. The group's first move, on 16 June, was to Camp Kilmer, New Jersey, for two weeks of processing, security lectures and rowdy parties. On 1 July the men moved out and boarded the *Queen Elizabeth* in New York Harbor.

OVERSEAS TO BODNEY

The *Queen Elizabeth*, with personnel from the 352nd FG aboard, sailed out of New York Harbor during the night of 30 June 1943, and six days later entered the Firth of Clyde, in Scotland. The following day the men of the 352nd boarded a train bound for England. Approximately 24 hours later the train stopped at a little town called Watton, in East Anglia. The group's initial home was at a permanent airfield located a mile from Watton, and the men were wild with joy after seeing the brick buildings and paved roads. The 486th FS's diary noted;

'This couldn't be for us. We never had anything so good in the States. Much to our regret, we soon found out that it was only a temporary set-up, and that our permanent base would be at Bodney, five miles away.'

The 352nd FG's new home was located in the rolling, wooded area of East Anglia midway between the towns of Norwich and King's Lynn. The airfield was grass-surfaced, and encircled by a paved perimeter road. Its previous tenants, the Royal Air Force, had improved the base by building 26 hardstands in the woods surrounding the field, as well as technical facilities on the western side of the base. However, even with these prior improvements, the airfield was not completely ready for occupancy, and for the next few days 352nd personnel commuted from Watton to finish the preparations. When the additional work was completed, the men of the 352nd FG, less the pilots, moved into Nissen huts at Bodney.

The pilots, due to a shortage of billets on the base, were 'forced' to move into a nearby manor house named Clermont Hall, and they loved it. As it turned out their life of luxury was to be cruelly cut short by a visit from an Air Inspector to Bodney, who declared that the pilots were too far from their aircraft to respond to an alert. His ultimatum abruptly ended their stay in Clermont Hall. Group CO, Lt Col Joe Mason, was less than impressed by the order to move his pilots, 'Mac' McCarthy stating;

'The Colonel felt that the pilots were at less risk to colds and other respiratory diseases which might ground them if they could stay in the warmth of the mansion, rather than the eternally cold Nissen huts.'

Below
Brand new P-47D-5 42-8660 of the 328th FS sits on the hardstanding at Bodney in August 1943. Note that it has the red surround to the national insignia but as yet no code letters – the letters 'PE-D' would soon be applied. The fighter was assigned to Lt Harry Miller, and he named it *Jean Louise*. He claimed his sole aerial victory (a Bf 110) in this Thunderbolt on 20 February 1944 (*352nd FG Association*)

Bottom
Bill Halton's P-47D-5 42-8439 *Slender, Tender and Tall* was also photographed in August 1943. Like Miller, Halton claimed a kill (a Bf 109) on 20 February 1944 using this machine (*352nd FG Association*)

Capt Dick DeBruin gives a 'one-finger salute' as he poses with Bill Halton's P-47D-5, which now also boasts a 'gunslinging' *Bugs Bunny* artwork (*Richard DeBruin*)

***Slender, Tender and Tall* once again, this time acting as a platform for its pilot, future 10.5-kill ace Bill Halton, and Hollywood film star Capt Clark Gable. This unique photograph was taken during Gable's stay at Bodney in August 1943, the actor fronting a film unit that was documenting the activities of a typical fighter group in the ETO (*352nd FG Association*)**

Shortly after the 352nd settled in at Bodney the group's first few P-47s arrived, and the pilots began flying training missions. On the ground, meanwhile, the administrative and maintenance crews continued to prepare the group for its combat role. In the first weeks groundcrews were hindered by the late arrival of some of their equipment, although they still managed to support the flying programme by readying each new aircraft for combat operations. By mid-August the 352nd had received its full complement of Thunderbolts, and training was progressing well.

During this period Capt Clark Gable and his film crew arrived at Bodney to shoot the 352nd FG's activities for use in documentaries he was preparing for the home front. Gable's visit was a real morale booster for the group, and a truly memorable occasion for the men of Bodney.

By early September the 352nd FG had completed its training, and the group was declared combat ready. The call to duty was not long in coming, and on 9 September 1943 40 P-47s departed from Bodney and headed towards the North Sea coast. The group, led by Lt Col Mason, was to patrol the English coastline from Southwold to Felixstowe, and cover the landings of the 56th and 353rd FGs as they returned from an escort mission. The mission was totally uneventful, but according to Ralph Hamilton of the 487th FS, 'it was a real confidence builder'. A second operation planned for the day was recalled because of poor weather.

As was customary during a new fighter group's breaking-in period, VIII Fighter Command sent an experienced combat leader to Bodney to lead the 352nd on its first sweeps into enemy territory. The tutor assigned to the group was Lt Col Harry Dayhuff of the 78th FG, based at Duxford, and he led the 352nd FG on its first intrusion over 'Fortress Europe' on 14 September 1943. Two missions were flown that day, and the 352nd suffered its first operational loss during the second mission. The group had performed fighter sweeps into Belgium on both occasions, and the missions had proven to be uneventful. The Luftwaffe was nowhere to be seen, and even the flak gunners held their fire, but fate stepped in and the 486th FS's Lt William Alm disappeared. His P-47D-2 (42-22531) was last seen 50 miles south of Felixstowe, and it almost certainly crashed into the sea due to mechanical failure.

Looking very pleased with himself, Lt Ralph Hamilton poses with his P-47D-2 42-22457 *Frances B* after flying the 352nd's first mission on 9 September 1943. He would complete a further 129 missions before ending his tour in the ETO in March 1945, by which time he had claimed four aircraft shot down (*352nd FG Association*)

This was the group's second fatality in 24 hours, for Lt Arthur Eaker of the 328th FS had been killed in a flying accident on the 13th.

After leading the 352nd on three more missions during the period of 15-22 September, Harry Dayhuff declared the group combat ready and returned operational control to Lt Col Mason. During the remainder of September the 352nd flew only four missions, and these passed without incident except for minor flak damage being inflicted to a solitary P-47.

The lack of enemy action during September 1943 was not an indication that the 352nd had been despatched against soft targets, because other groups in VIII Fighter Command had also failed to encounter the enemy.

Formerly CO of the 78th FG's 82nd FS, Lt Col Harry Dayhuff was assigned to the 352nd FG during its 'breaking in' period in the ETO. A highly experienced P-47 pilot, he led the group on its first four missions in September 1943, before returning to the 78th FG's HQ flight at Duxford. Dayhuff rotated home in April 1944 (*via Sam Sox*)

The primary reason for this lull in action was that the Luftwaffe's high command had realised that escorted bombing raids over the Reich were becoming a major threat, and had begun to realign the defensive zones for its fighters. Most notable was the reassignment of a number of its coastal defence units to bases in Germany. Additionally, the Luftwaffe had transferred units from the Mediterranean and Russian theatres back home.

The Luftwaffe introduced its new defence in depth strategy on 27 September, but its airmen received a very unpleasant surprise when they encountered USAAF escort fighters, carrying belly tanks, over Emden. The startled defenders were bounced by a large and unexpected formation of fighters, and 21 German aircraft fell in flames. This defeat resulted in further readjustments by the Luftwaffe, and for the most part its fighters disappeared from the skies for the next few missions.

Inspirational leader of the 352nd FG, Lt Col Joe 'Red Dog' Mason flew P-47D-5 42-8466 from the autumn of 1943 through to the spring of 1944. During this time he claimed his first kill (a Bf 109G) in the fighter on 24 February 1944. As this photograph clearly shows, Mason had his P-47 personalised with the badge of the 59th FS (with whom he had previously served) and the sobriquet *"GENA THIS IS IT"*. The Thunderbolt had originally been christened *THIS IS IT*, and *GENA* was hastily added after Mason wrote to his wife telling her that he had named his P-47 after her. She in turn asked to see a photo of it, and the machine's nickname had to modified to avoid Col Mason's blushes! (*via Sam Sox*)

Following a brief break, German fighters were up in force during the missions of 8 and 10 October, and VIII Fighter Command pilots exacted a toll from their ranks on each occasion. On the second of these two missions the 352nd finally got the opportunity to fire its guns at enemy fighters during a brief encounter with some Bf 109s near Hertogenbosch, in Holland. The first claim was filed by future seven-kill ace Capt Willie O Jackson of the 486th FS, who reported that he damaged and possibly destroyed a Bf 109 near Cleves. Sadly, Lt Fred Olson of the 328th lost his life when he crashed his battle-damaged P-47D-5 42-8635 into the Channel on the way home.

This encounter ended the 352nd's contact with the Luftwaffe until late November 1943. During the intervening weeks, several major air battles did take place, but the action always seemed to occur in sectors other than the one being patrolled by the 352nd FG. Those VIII Fighter Command units that did encounter the Luftwaffe during this period noted a major change in its tactics, with the mission of 14 October 1943 (which later became known as 'Black Thursday') being particularly significant.

On this date German single-engined fighters met and engaged the escorts just after they crossed the coastline of Europe. While the USAAF fighters were busy fending off these attacks, the unescorted bombers continued on to the targets in Schweinfurt and Regensburg, where they were badly mauled by twin-engined interceptors. No less than 60 bombers were lost, while only 13 claims were made by US fighter pilots in return. This mission graphically illustrated that the Eighth Air Force had to escort its bombers all the way to and from the target.

A partial solution to the problem was realised when the first two P-38 groups went into action during early November 1943. The long range Lockheed fighter at last gave VIII Fighter Command the ability to protect the bombers all the way to Germany and back. The die was now cast, and the battle for control of the skies over Western Europe was about to begin.

The period of 5-25 November was particularly frustrating for the 352nd because numerous battles took place and VIII Fighter Command pilots claimed a total of 42 destroyed, nine probably destroyed and 29 damaged. As in October, the group's sector always seemed to be away from the scene of battle, as the mission of 25 November clearly showed. On this day, the 352nd flew a fighter sweep to France in the hope of engaging the Luftwaffe, but again the enemy was nowhere in sight. To make matters even worse, intense flak was encountered in the Dunkirk-Calais area and one P-47 was slightly damaged. Twenty-six missions had now been flown and the 352nd FG had yet to claim a confirmed victory.

On 10 October 1943 Capt Willie O Jackson of the 486th FS became the first pilot in the 352nd FG to engage and damage an enemy aircraft. Later to lead both the 328th and 486th FSs during a 104-mission tour that lasted until war's end, Jackson would be credited with the destruction of seven aircraft confirmed, one probably destroyed and three damaged in the air, as well as four strafing victories (*Sheldon Berlow*)

Lt Leo Northrup crash-landed his P-47D-5 42-8491 *Donna Dae III* near Bodney at the end of a bomber escort mission to Germany on 5 November 1943. He subsequently flew both a P-51B and a P-51D christened *Donna Dae* during his ETO tour, which ended in August 1944. Northrup scored two aerial kills (Bf 109Gs) with the 352nd, on 21 June 1944, east of Warsaw during the Eighth Air Force's first 'Shuttle Mission' to Russia (*352nd FG Association*)

'THE FIRST OF THE MANY'

Mission number 27 took place on 26 November, and it was Maj John Meyer's 487th FS that found itself involved in the opening round. The group's mission on this day was to provide withdrawal support for the bombers returning from a raid on Bremen. The rendezvous with a mixed formation of B-17s and B-24s was made at 27,000 ft in the vicinity of Strücklingen, where the group found that the B-17s were maintaining good formation, but the B-24s had become spread out, offering the German fighters some easy targets. The predicted attack was not long in coming, and the engagement began as the bombers neared Gröningen. Six Bf 109s dived down and attacked two straggling B-24s, and they in turn were bounced by Maj Meyer and Yellow Flight of the 487th FS.

In the ensuing battle three of the Bf 109s were shot out of the sky, the first German fighter to be confirmed destroyed by the 352nd FG going down under a hail of gunfire from 'J C' Meyer's P-47D-5 42-8529 *LAMBIE*. Moments later he claimed a second Bf 109 as a probable. Maj Meyer's encounter report stated;

'As the enemy aircraft started to Chandelle upwards for another pass (at the B-24) I closed to within 300 yards of him and fired a burst using about ten degrees deflection. The enemy aircraft, which I identified as an Me 109F or G with "rocket guns" (210 mm rockets – Editor) slung under his wings, exploded with a large burst of flame and disintegrated in the air. Fragments flew past me in my turn and struck and damaged Yellow 4, flown by Maj Therriault. At this moment another enemy aircraft came into my sights.

'He was turning away from me, but I had no difficulty turning inside of him. I took a wide two ring shot at him using about 45 degrees of deflection, which placed him out of sight below the fuselage of my ship, so I saw nothing that followed. Maj Ross, flying Yellow 2, saw this aircraft give off large quantities of smoke from the right side of its cowling. At this moment I was attacked from above and to the right by another

Maj John C 'Whips' Meyer is helped with his straps by his crew chief, S/Sgt William Conkey, as he settles into the cockpit of *LAMBIE* (P-47D-5 42-8529) in preparation for another mission. Long-time CO of the 487th FS, and later deputy group CO of the 352nd FG, Brooklyn-born Meyer claimed all three of his Thunderbolt kills (and a solitary probable) with this machine in November-December 1943 (*352nd FG Association*)

enemy aircraft, so I continued my turn very steeply and found myself head-on to him. I fired a short burst head-on at point blank range, but saw no hits on him.'

Capt Donald K Dilling then attacked Meyer's assailant, and with several well placed bursts from his 'fifties', sent it heading straight down trailing a heavy column of black smoke. The third and final kill of the day was shared by Lts John Bennett and Robert Berkshire.

After an uneventful mission on 29 November, the group returned to Germany the next day and suffered its heaviest losses to date. As the 352nd penetrated the enemy coast, bombers of the 1st Bomb Division were seen coming toward them. Evidently this bomber force had aborted its mission and was on the way out. Nevertheless, the 352nd continued on to its rendezvous point and duly made several orbits in the area. Whilst circling near Neerpelt, in Belgium, Green and Blue Flights of the 486th FS were bounced by approximately five Bf 109s from 34,000 ft.

In the following melee three Thunderbolt pilots, Lts Robert Babbitt, Robert Brown and David Kramer, were shot down by the Messerschmitts – Babbitt and Brown were killed and Kramer was posted Missing in Action, although he subsequently evaded capture and returned to the UK. One Bf 109 was reportedly seen going down trailing smoke, but no claims were filed by any of the returning 486th pilots. It is possible that one of the missing pilots succeeded in destroying this enemy aircraft before being hit.

Immediately after this encounter the 2nd Task Force, and its escort, were seen heading towards the 352nd formation, so the group joined up with them and escorted the bombers to Woerth, on the Franco-German border, before breaking off. Just as the 352nd FG left the bombers, it became involved in a strange dogfight. Capt Hayes Button of the 487th saw a P-38 with 'old style' US markings attacking some P-47s, so he bounced it. Button's gunfire set one engine ablaze, and he then flew alongside the P-38 for a better look. By the time he came around for a second pass, the Lightning had disappeared from view. Capt Dilling also reported a second mysterious P-38 that carried no national insignia, but did not attack.

Things were grim at Bodney upon their return, especially in the 486th FS. The 352nd had just taken its worst pounding of its short operational life, and the loss of three pilots from one squadron was extremely painful.

Revenge was not long in coming. On 1 December the 352nd's assignment was to escort the bombers of the 1st Bomb Division back to England. Rendezvous was made over Holland

Although of indifferent quality, the rarity of this photograph more than qualifies it for inclusion. This P-47D wears the code 'LA-F', denoting that it was one of several similarly-marked Thunderbolts flown by pilots of HQ VIII Fighter Command who accompanied the 352nd on some of its early missions in the autumn of 1943. The serial of this particular fighter remains unknown, and the rarely seen 'LA' code had disappeared by the early spring of 1944. Other 'LA'-coded P-47s were operated by the 2906th (provisional) Fighter Training Group at Atcham, in Shropshire (*352nd FG Association*)

in the vicinity of Rheydt, and the main force of bombers was found to be in a good tight formation. This meant that it was being virtually ignored by the German fighters, who were instead concentrating on a number of stragglers. The 487th FS was the first unit to observe the German attackers, and it peeled off after them. Pacific War combat veteran Capt George Preddy quickly bounced a Bf 109, setting it on fire with his first burst and then watching it blow up following a second longer burst. He had just scored the first of his eventual 26.833 kills.

In an almost simultaneous action, Lt Virgil Meroney attacked another Bf 109 and saw its pilot bail out after hitting it with a long burst. Meroney then turned his attention to a twin-engined 'Me 210' (almost certainly an Me 410), which was flying a straight course. After two passes the enemy aircraft was seriously damaged by Meroney's gunfire, and it was finished off by Lt Richard Grow, who forced the two-man crew to take to their parachutes.

Three days later, on 4 December, the 352nd headed back to Holland on a fighter sweep, and the pilots were hoping to 'mix it up' with the German fighters. The Luftwaffe proved to be quite accommodating in this respect, and it met the 352nd FG shortly after the group had made landfall over

Boasting individual canvas canopy and engine covers to help keep out the all-pervading winter dampness, these Thunderbolts of the 487th FS have been 'put to bed' for the night at Bodney in late December 1943. The nearest P-47D-5 is 42-8516 'HO-Z', named *Lucky Boy*, which was the first assigned fighter of Lt Carl Luksic. He later claimed 8.5 kills with the P-51B prior to being downed by flak over Germany and captured on 24 May 1944 (*352nd FG Association*)

This photograph, taken in early December 1943, features Capt George Preddy's first Thunderbolt in the ETO, P-47D-5 42-8500. He flew this aircraft from September 1943 through to April 1944, although he never claimed a kill in it. The cross marked below the cockpit of the fighter denotes Preddy's first victory (a Bf 109), which he scored on 1 December 1943 whilst flying Lt Ralph Hamilton's P-47D-2 42-22457 *Frances B* (see photo on page 12). His next victory (an 'Me 210') came on 22 December, and this time he was at the controls of Lt Virgil Meroney's P-47D-5 42-8473 *Sweet LOUISE*. Finally, on 29 January 1944 Preddy claimed an Fw 190 flying Lt John Bennett's P-47D-5 42-8421 – he was shot down by flak in this machine on the same mission, bailing out over the Channel. *Cripes A'Mighty* derived its nickname from the phrase that Preddy yelled when he released the dice whilst playing craps! Note the fighter's striped wheel covers and highly polished gun barrels (*William Kohlhas*)

Lt Clarence Palmer's P-47D-2 42-8007 *HELEN OF TROY* suffered a collapsed starboard undercarriage leg after experiencing a rough landing at Bodney in early October 1943. Palmer was issued with P-47D-2 42-8382 as a replacement, which he proceeded to fly until the 487th FS converted to P-51Bs in the spring of 1944. A veteran of 85 missions (and the scorer of two aerial kills and one strafing victory) by the time he left the ETO in August 1944, all of Palmer's Thunderbolts and Mustangs were christened *HELEN OF TROY* (*352nd FG Association*)

the Dutch coast. The 328th FS engaged the enemy first, but the skirmish ended in a 'scoreless draw'.

The German pilots then engaged the 487th FS, and they quickly realised that they had made a grave mistake. Maj John C Meyer disposed of the first Bf 109 with only one burst, and as his White Flight broke away, Yellow Flight took up the action. Flying as Yellow 3, Lt Meroney saw two Bf 109s heading towards them, so he turned to counter their attack. As one of the German fighters dived away, Meroney gave chase, and with two well placed bursts he set the Messerschmitt alight and sent it crashing into a farmhouse. After becoming separated from their flight, Meroney and his wingman joined up with Blue Flight from the 328th.

As they approached the P-47s Lt Meroney saw a Fw 190 settling in behind Blue 4, so he in turn fell in behind the unsuspecting German. His gunfire gravely damaged the Focke-Wulf fighter, and as it fell away Lt J L Sweeney put a few rounds into it for good measure. With a kill and a shared victory following this mission, future nine-kill ace Virgil Meroney raised his total to three, thus becoming the 352nd's top scorer to date.

After an uneventful mission on 5 December, the 352nd FG, like the remainder of VIII Fighter Command, stood down for nearly a week. Then on the 11th 388 fighters headed for the Continent as escorts for three bomb divisions sent to attack Emden. The Luftwaffe was up in force, and in a vigorous defence of its territory, lost 21 of its fighters. The bulk of the claims were filed by the veteran 56th FG, although the 352nd was able to chip in with two confirmed kills. The first victory of the day was scored by Capt Don Dilling of the 487th, who downed a twin-engined Bf 110. Ten minutes later Lt Ray Cornick claimed the 328th FS's first confirmed kill by destroying a second Messerschmitt *Zerstörer*.

Things went a little quiet after this successful engagement, and only one mission was flown during the course of the next eight days. Finally, on

Most fighter squadrons had an unofficial artist whose job it was to adorn aircraft with (predominantly 'girlie') nose art. The 486th FS had Nilan Jones, and a fine example of his handiwork is seen here on squadron CO Maj Luther Richmond's P-47D-5 42-8412 *"Sweetie"*. Immediately behind this aircraft is P-47D-5 42-8699 *PRAIRIE FARMER/ SPIRIT OF LOS ANGELES CITY COLLEGE*, which was assigned to nine-kill ace Capt Stephen Andrew. A combat veteran from the Pacific theatre (where he had downed a Zero flying a P-40E with the 49th FG from Darwin, Australia, in April 1942), Andrew claimed his first ETO kill (a Bf 109) with 42-8699 on 15 March 1944. His remaining seven victories were all scored in P-51Bs. Returning to 42-8699, what appears to be a white line beneath the canopy is the fighter's name, *PRAIRIE FARMER/SPIRIT OF LOS ANGELES CITY COLLEGE* (*352nd FG Association*)

20 December the weather improved enough for the Eighth Air Force to go back into action. The target was Bremen, and the attack was carried out in magnificent style. Indeed, the escort fighters performed their assignments so well that the mission was later officially documented as a perfect example of how bombers should be protected in enemy skies.

The attack was carried out by ten combat wings of bombers, and they were escorted all the way by fighters. Nine P-47 groups covered the 'heavies' to the target area IP (Initial Point), where they were relieved by the longer ranged P-38s and P-51s, which took them to the target and back. German fighters were encountered throughout the mission and VIII Fighter Command pilots destroyed 19, probably destroyed three and damaged six. Five American aircraft also were lost in the day's engagements.

The 352nd FG accounted for six of the 19 kills scored that day, encountering the Luftwaffe on two separate occasions. The first action took place just as the 486th FS made its rendezvous with the bombers. Blue Flight was bounced by a solitary Bf 109, which closed in on the tail of Lt Alfred Marshall's P-47. However, before its daring pilot could open fire, Capt Franklyn Greene forced him to break off. He then followed the fleeing Messerschmitt and set it on fire with a well-aimed burst. The crippled Bf 109 spiralled earthward out of control, and Capt Greene became the first pilot in the 486th FS to down an enemy aircraft.

After this engagement the 352nd continued its escort without incident until reaching Friesoythe where, as the group was breaking off to return to Bodney, the 487th's Capt Dilling observed a gaggle of bandits attacking a B-17. After alerting his squadron, Dilling led the attack and quickly sent a Bf 109 down in flames for his third (and last) victory. Minutes later four more German fighters were shot down by Capt Winfield E McIntyre and Lts Clayton Davis, Daniel Britt and Harold S Riley, all of whom were

The 486th FS's Capt Franklyn Greene decided that the P-47s in his flight would be named after *Snow White and the Seven Dwarfs*. Greene's P-47D-2 42-22509 was named ***SNOW WHITE*** and wore the code letters 'PZ-I' (*352nd FG Association*)

Capt Donald Dilling of the 487th FS poses with his ***QUEEN CITY MAMA*** (P-47D-5 42-8447) a few days before he crash-landed it in occupied France. Dilling scored all three of his victories in this aircraft (*Donald Dilling*)

from the 487th. After blunting the enemy attack, the squadron escorted the heavily damaged Flying Fortress back across the English Channel.

Following a one-day stand-down, the 352nd FG returned to Germany on 22 December as part of the escort for bombers coming back from an attack on Osnabrück and Münster. The Luftwaffe again carried out a stubborn defence of its homeland, losing more of its fighter force in the process. The 352nd played a major role in this mission, its pilots claiming six destroyed, one probably destroyed and three damaged out of VIII Fighter Command's overall total of 15 destroyed, one probably destroyed and six damaged.

German fighters had bounced the 'heavies' just as the 487th FS assumed its position alongside the bomber stream. In the ensuing engagement three enemy aircraft went down, the first (a Bf 109G) being destroyed by Maj John C Meyer, who 'bagged' the leader of the attacking formation after a lengthy dogfight. Next, Lts John Bennett and Ernest McMahon shared in the destruction of a second Bf 109, with the former following this up by damaging a third Messerschmitt fighter. His squadronmate, Lt Harold Riley, then claimed yet another Bf 109 as a probable. The third 487th FS victory was scored by Capt George Preddy, who destroyed an 'Me 210' after evading two attacks by Bf 109s. Unfortunately, Preddy's

Maj Everett Stewart, CO of the 328th FS, poses with his P-47D-5 42-8437 *Sunny IV*. Coded 'PE-G', the aircraft was used by Stewart to claim a half-share in a Bf 110 destroyed on 22 December 1943 with Lt Robert H 'Punchy' Powell, as well as an 'Me 210' damaged on the same mission. Stewart was later credited with 0.333 of a kill with 42-8437 on 5 January 1944 when he and Lts John Coleman and 'Punchy' Powell destroyed an He 177. A further seven kills would be credited to Stewart whilst flying the P-51B. One of only a handful of pilots to serve command postings with three fighter groups in the ETO, Stewart was CO of the 328th FS upon the 352nd FG's arrival in England. He was then posted to the 355th FG as its Executive Officer in January 1944. Made CO of the Steeple Morden-based group ten months later, Stewart was subsequently sent to lead the 4th FG in February 1945. He remained here until September of that year. Prior to his time in the ETO, Stewart had already completed a tour of duty in the Pacific with the 20th PG – which included being at Pearl Harbor on 7 December 1941! All of this frontline flying meant that 'Ev' Stewart participated in no less than 180 combat missions, totalling 510 hours of 'stick time', during World War 2 (*Sheldon Berlow*)

wingman, Lt Richard Grow, lost his life while protecting his leader from an attack by one of these Bf 109s. The final moments of Grow's life were recorded in George Preddy's encounter report;

'Lt Grow called that a Me 109 was on my tail. I threw the stick in the left corner (of the cockpit) and saw the enemy aircraft behind me and out of range. I continued down, skidding and slipping. Grow then called that an enemy aircraft was on his tail, but I was unable to locate him. I told Grow to hit the deck, then I went into a cloud and set course for home on instruments. I stayed in the clouds for about 15 minutes and broke out over the Dutch coast at 3000 ft. I could not contact Lt Grow and did not see him again.'

The 328th FS also encountered more German fighters as the formation neared the Dutch town of Zwolle, and White Flight, led by Maj Everett Stewart, claimed three Bf 110s destroyed and one 'Me 210' damaged in the ensuing dogfight. Lts John B Coleman and Francis Horne each downed a Bf 110, while the third Bf 110 was shared by Maj Stewart and Lt Robert H Powell Jr.

During the next few days the 352nd FG was relatively inactive, and this break was welcomed by the group for it gave its personnel a chance to relax during its first Holiday Season at Bodney. The festivities came to an end on 30 December, however, when the 352nd's 38th combat mission turned out to be something of a nightmare for the 487th FS.

As the group (led by Col Joe Mason) arrived over the enemy coastline, it encountered poor weather conditions. Despite this, the 352nd continued on to the rendezvous point, flying above a solid overcast. It duly met up with its assigned bomber formation ten minutes late, and as the group flew across France a shark-mouthed Bf 110 was observed flying parallel to the bombers. Pilots from the 328th FS quickly despatched the lone *Zerstörer*, this kill (shared between Lt Col Eugene 'Pop' Clark and Lts David Hendrian and David Zims) being the only high point in the mission.

Things began to go awry when the 487th FS, which was already concerned about its fuel situation, broke off escort near Calais and headed back to base. As the unit approached the Channel it was attacked by three Fw 190s, and the P-47 pilots evaded the bounce by diving away into the heavy mist. As the US fighters entered the overcast, the enemy aircraft broke off their attack so as to allow the flak gunners along the French coast

Lt Murdock 'Scottie' Cunningham and his crew check over his P-47D-5 42-8460 *The Flying Scot!* in preparation for another mission. Note the flight jacket bearing the painting of 'Grumpy', one of the *Seven Dwarfs*. Cunningham completed his tour in the ETO in June 1944, finishing with one aerial victory and 1.5 strafing kills to his credit (*352nd FG Association*)

Lt Chester 'Chet' Harker and his crew chief, S/Sgt Charles Agee, with their P-47D-2 42-22486 *"Cile"/Luck of the Irish*. Harker served with the 486th FS from 1943 through to the end of the war (*Chester Harker*)

to open fire with a deadly barrage. During their attempt to evade intense ground fire some of the pilots became disoriented in fog, and three of the 487th FS's senior men – Capts Donald Dilling, Hayes Button and Winfield McIntyre – ran out of fuel and came down in occupied France.

Dilling managed to evade capture and was eventually returned to England, but Hayes and McIntyre were quickly caught, and they would spend the rest of the war as PoWs. At the time of his loss, Capt Dilling was tied with Maj John Meyer and Lt Virgil Meroney as the 352nd's high scorers.

As 1943 came to a close, the 352nd FG, after a slow start, had developed into a superb fighting unit. It was now ready to play its part in the major air battles that would become a feature of 1944. The learning curve had been a tough one, for in the 38 missions that the group had undertaken, its pilots had destroyed 22 enemy aircraft for the loss of ten of their own. Five men had been killed in action and one in an operational training accident, two had become PoWs and two had evaded capture, one of whom eventually made it back to Bodney.

VIII Fighter Command's mission for 1944 was to establish aerial superiority over Europe, and to accomplish this goal the pilots were instructed to strike the enemy wherever they found him, in the air or on the ground. Under these new guidelines fighter pilots, after completing their escort duties (and if fuel allowed), could search out aircraft or ground targets and attack them. As an added incentive, VIII Fighter Command announced that its pilots would receive full victory credits for aircraft destroyed on the ground.

A NEW ERA IN FIGHTER ESCORT

Aside from being cleared to attack German targets away from the bomber stream, the fighter groups were also informed of changes to the standard escort tactics that would also be implemented come the New Year. Previously, a group would rendezvous with the bombers and stay with the 'big friends' until relieved. Now, a group would be assigned to a certain area of the bomber route, and would patrol it until the bombers had passed through.

The new tactics were put into use in the first week of January 1944, and proved quite successful. The mission of 5 January saw over 500 bombers despatched to four separate targets and losses were relatively light –

This P-47D-5 (42-8657), coded 'PE-K', was shared by the 328th's Lt Jamie Laing and Robert H 'Punchy' Powell Jr. In this photograph, 'Punchy' poses with his 'side of the aeroplane', which featured the name *THE WEST "by Gawd" VIRGINIAN*, as well as a map of the pilot's home state. Laing's 'side of the aeroplane' was named *Jamie my Boy* (*Robert H Powell Jr*)

Taken at around the same time as the previous shot, 'Punchy' Powell has been joined by his groundcrew for this photograph (*via Michael O'Leary*)

24 'heavies' were posted Missing in Action. Thirty German aircraft were downed by American fighters, but at a cost of 12 of their own.

Pilots of the 328th FS claimed the day's most unusual kill, a Heinkel He 177 bomber, which was shot down near La Ferté-Bernard, in France, by the combined efforts of Maj Everett Stewart and Lts Robert Powell and John Coleman. This was the first example of the Luftwaffe's largest bomber to be shot down by VIII Fighter Command, and the pilots involved all received a written commendation for their work. This victory was, however, the last the 352nd FG would score until 29 January.

Maj Harold Lund (right), CO of the 328th FS, and an unidentified member of his groundcrew sit atop their P-47D-5 42-8481 *Muriel V*. Coded 'PE-L', this machine was flown by Pacific Theatre veteran Lund until replaced by a P-51B in mid April 1944 (*USAF*)

The 328th FS's Capt Donald S Bryan with his P-47D-2 42-8381 *Little One*, whose name had obviously been applied by the same artist that had decorated Maj Lund's Thunderbolt. The fighter's mission board shows that the photograph was taken after Bryan had completed his 53rd combat sortie. *Little One* also displayed four kill markings under the canopy at this time. Bryan, who would finish his tour with the 352nd FG as CO of the 328th FS (having scored 13.333 kills), claimed his first 3.833 kills with 42-8381 (*USAF*)

There was a change of command in the 328th FS on 27 January when Maj Harold Lund replaced Everett Stewart as commanding officer. The newly promoted Lt Col Stewart departed the 352nd to become the Executive Officer of the 355th FG.

The day prior to the 328th FS's change of CO, tragedy had struck the 487th FS when Lt Lester Lowry dived into the ground near Bodney while on a local training flight in P-47D-5 42-8516. Lowry, who had only joined the group earlier in the month, was killed.

The 352nd FG's scoring drought was broken during the mission to Frankfurt on 29 January, when its pilots scored six confirmed kills. The victorious pilots were Capt George Preddy and Lts Virgil Meroney, Clayton Davis and William T Whisner (all of whom would become aces) of the 487th FS and Lt John Coleman of the 328th FS. The sixth victory of the mission was shared by Lts Don Bryan and Quentin Quinn of the 328th.

The day's success was not without cost, however, as Lt Joel McPherson of HQ 352nd FG ran out of fuel over France and Capt Preddy had to bail out over the Channel after his fighter was struck by flak. Following a short stay 'in the drink', Preddy was retrieved by an air-sea rescue Walrus and returned to Bodney. McPherson would also eventually return to the UK, but not before he had fought alongside the French Maquis (resistance), been captured by the Germans, and then escaped once again!

In a sad post-script to the combat losses, that same day Group Flight Surgeon Nathan Nyland and enlisted men Sgt Joseph Rubin and Pvt Floyd Ernest (from the Medical Section of the 487th FS) were killed when the B-24 that they were flying in locally caught fire and crashed.

The 352nd continued its scoring ways on 30 January. As the group arrived at its rendezvous point, the bombers were already under attack by a mixed force of single- and twin-engined fighters. Yellow Flight of the 328th FS rushed in to break up the attack and Lts Jack Thornell, Bill Schwenke and John Walker quickly downed three enemy aircraft. Fifteen minutes later Blue Flight of the 328th, led by Lt Don Bryan, engaged two Fw 190s, and shot them out of the sky. One of the kills was credited to Bryan, and the other was shared by Lts Quentin Quinn and Francis Horne. Capt Edward Gignac and Lt Alfred Marshall of the 486th FS then joined the fray and added a Bf 110 to the victory list.

The final kills of the day were credited to Lts Robert Ross and Virgil Meroney of the 487th FS, with the latter pilot's solitary Bf 109 being of particular significance, for this was Meroney's fifth confirmed victory. He was now the 352nd FG's first ace, and he reported his kill as follows;

'Leading Crown Prince Blue Flight, I turned into 12+ Me 109s approaching from seven o'clock at 30,000 ft and made a head-on pass at the nearest one, firing one short burst from 400 yards and 10-15 degrees of deflection. I observed a few hits but did not see what became of him.

'I then made a fast 180-degree turn and chased a flight of four enemy aircraft. I went after the nearest one, firing short bursts as I closed from 400 yards to 150 yards. My last burst was as he was going straight down at 10,000 ft. The right wing came off and the aircraft disintegrated. I had no trouble staying with the Me 109, and could overtake him at will. I pulled up and joined some other P-47s, as my flight had separated.'

After this mission the 352nd stood down until 3 February, when it headed for Emden. Nearing the target, three Fw 190s tried to bounce the 487th FS, but Virgil Meroney cut off their approach and destroyed one of them in a diving attack for his sixth victory. However, the 328th FS did

Lt Harold Nussman of the 328th FS, posing with his P-47D-5 42-8515 *Dixie Boy*, was killed in action on 8 February 1944 while flying P-47D-5 42-8419 *Blondie*. *Dixie Boy*, coded 'PE-N', was in turn reassigned to Lt Raymond Phillips. who renamed it *Hildegard*. He did, however, retain the same code letters (*352nd FG Association*)

not fare as well in its encounter with the Luftwaffe, losing Lt Ray Cornick in aerial combat. Lt Joseph Sweeney later crashed into the North Sea when his P-47 ran out of fuel returning to Bodney. Both men were killed.

The 328th FS revenged its losses of the previous day when German fighters were engaged in two separate dogfights over Belgium. Three Fw 190s were destroyed and two damaged, Lts John Walker Jr, Francis Horne and Fremont Miller each being credited with one kill, and damage credits going to Lts Frederick Yochim and Marion V Long. A solitary P-47D-5 (42-8680), piloted by Lt Wendell Parlee, was so badly damaged in the melee that its pilot was forced to crash-land at Manston.

Ill fortune again struck the 328th FS on 8 February when three of its pilots were killed while escorting a crippled B-17, and two others staggered back to Bodney in crippled P-47s. Killed in the attack by Fw 190s were Lts John Walker, James Meager and Harold Nussman.

The target for 10 February was Brunswick, in Germany, and 466 fighters from the VIII and IX Fighter Commands escorted 169 B-17s of the 3rd Bomb Division to the target and back. German fighters were also up in force, and aggressively engaged the American formations from the Dutch coast to the target and back. The Luftwaffe suffered heavy losses in the battle, with 56 fighters being claimed destroyed and another 40 damaged against American losses of nine fighters and 29 bombers.

The air action was at times confusing, resulting in low claims by the 352nd. In one engagement eleven P-51s from another group forced their way into the 487th's designated patrol area, causing the P-47 pilots to cease firing. In spite of the mix-up, Virgil Meroney was able to down a Bf 109 for his seventh kill, and future seven-kill ace Lt Walter Starck flamed another for his first victory. His encounter report read in part;

'He was taking terrific evasive action, but as I closed on him I saw hits all around his fuselage and wing roots. The enemy aircraft started pouring smoke and white vapour. He suddenly stopped his evasive action, and as I pulled away at 14,000 ft, he went down in a straight dive, taking no evasive action whatsoever.'

Bad weather returned the next day, and it remained nasty for much of the following week. Finally, on 20 February, the skies cleared and the Eighth Air Force initiated 'Big Week' by returning to Germany

Another of the 486th FS's 'Seven Dwarfs'. *DOPEY* (alias P-47D-5 42-8459), coded 'PZ-U', was piloted by Lt Lloyd A Rauk, and the aircraft also carried the name *Rauk-et* on its fuselage. Completing his ETO tour in August 1944, Rauk claimed two aerial kills flying the P-51 (*352nd FG Association*)

Lt Lawrence 'Mac' McCarthy used P-47D-5 42-26320 *Pattie II* to claim two Bf 110s destroyed on 20 February 1944. The fighter was coded 'PE-M' (*USAF*)

with a massive force of 1003 bombers and 832 fighters. The goal of 'Big Week' was to strike and destroy aircraft production facilities throughout Germany. The plan was two-fold. While the bombers blasted aircraft factories, the fighters would seek out and destroy German fighters in the air or on the ground.

VIII Fighter Command enjoyed great success on the opening day of the bomber offensive, with its pilots claiming 61 aircraft destroyed, seven probably destroyed and 37 damaged, all for the loss of just six fighters. A major contributor to these statistics was the 352nd FG, which claimed 12 destroyed, one probably destroyed and four damaged.

German fighters began an attack on the bomber stream just as the 352nd FG was taking up its position, and the 486th FS quickly bounced the enemy aircraft. Two separate engagements ensued as the 486th intercepted a gaggle of fighters in the rendezvous area. while the 328th FS fought a running battle across the entire withdrawal route. First blood was drawn by the latter unit when Lt Lawrence 'Mac' McCarthy charged into a flight of Bf 110s, shooting two out of the sky and damaging two others.

Moments later his squadronmates downed five more of the big twin-engined fighters in a one-sided battle, Lt Col Roy Osborne, Capt William T Halton and Lts Raymond Phillips and Henry Miller all being credited with single kills. The fifth Bf 110 fell to the combined firepower of Lt Col Osborne, Capt Don Bryan and Lt David Zims.

In the other dogfight Lt Frank Cutler out-fought two Bf 109s, which crashed near Nivelles, and then destroyed a Bf 110 on the ground. As Cutler's victims fell to earth, Maj Willie O Jackson and Lt Kenneth Williams further reduced the Luftwaffe's inventory by each downing a Bf 109 near Charleroi. Maj Jackson also damaged another Messerschmitt, and it was last seen limping home trailing smoke.

Major battles were again fought on 21 and 22 February, and German aircraft were destroyed in record numbers. However, all the action took place out of the 352nd's area of responsibility, and the group had to wait until the 24th before it 'mixed it up' with both aircraft and a ship.

The first encounter of the day took place near the German town of Schwagstorf, when Col Joe Mason, flying with the 328th FS, downed a Bf 109 and Don Bryan damaged a second. Five minutes later the 487th caught a flight of eight Bf 109s in the landing pattern over nearby Eschede airfield, and Lt Glennon Moran bounced the unsuspecting aircraft. His first target was hit by a short burst and plummeted to earth. As it crashed Moran damaged another Bf 109, and Lt Ralph Hamilton damaged a third, before the 487th disengaged from the attack and went home.

Following close behind the squadron was the 486th FS, which crossed the coastline near Egmond just as an E-Boat was being attacked by P-47s from another group. Lts Ed Heller, Alfred Marshall and Robert MacKean dived down to assist in the attack, and by the time they broke off and

resumed their course for home, the E-Boat, according to Ed Heller's report, 'Was dead in the water, listing, and smoking badly. It was not moving, and I assume it sank'.

In February 1944 a battle of a different sort was beginning in the Headquarters of the Eighth Air Force. This debate was over which groups in VIII Fighter Command would receive the coveted new Packard Merlin-engined P-51 Mustangs. The fiery Lt Col Don Blakeslee, CO of the 4th FG, was very upset that the first of the new P-51Bs had gone to a Ninth Air Force unit (354th FG), and he let his feelings be known. As a result, in late February 1944 the 4th FG became the first ETO-based Eighth Air Force unit to transition onto the Mustang.

The first P-51-equipped unit permanently assigned to the Eighth Air Force was the 357th FG, which had initially arrived in the UK in December 1943 as part of the Ninth Air Force. However, prior to being declared operational, the 357th was reassigned to the 'Mighty Eighth', which in turn transferred the P-47-equipped 356th FG to the Ninth Air Force. The 357th made its combat debut in early February 1944.

After another unit (355th FG) had received the next increment of Mustangs, group CO Col Joe Mason redoubled his efforts to obtain examples of the new fighter for the 352nd FG, and duly won his case. The first seven P-51Bs arrived on 1 March 1944, and were assigned to the 486th FS. A new era was now dawning at Bodney.

'Happy' the dwarf might have been pleased with his name, but the pilot of *HAPPY* the P-47 was most definitely not! Future 5.5-kill ace Lt Ed Heller pleaded with his flight commander, Capt Franklyn Greene, 'that Happy was not the name of a fighter plane'. This aircraft (P-47D-10 42-75183) was coded 'PZ-H' (*Edwin L Heller*)

Whenever possible, pilots would often select the initial letter of their surname as the identity of their assigned aircraft. This was the case with the 486th FS's P-47D-2 42-8377 'PZ-W', which was the personal mount of Lt Alton Wallace. Having joined the 352nd FG in the US prior to the group deploying to the ETO, Wallace was still serving in the front-line come VE-Day, by which time he had shot down three aircraft and destroyed a similar number on the ground. He completed 64 missions (*via Sam Sox*)

MUSTANG OPERATIONS BEGIN

Due to the limited supply of Mustangs in the ETO in early 1944, the 352nd FG was forced to endure a protracted conversion onto the type. Such problems had not afflicted the previous groups issued with the P-51B, the 4th and 355th FGs having almost fully transitioned to the fighter before they resumed operations, and the 357th receiving Mustangs prior to first seeing combat. With the 352nd, however, two-and-a-half units would still be flying the P-47 when the Mustang made its debut with the group on 8 March 1944. The 486th historian noted;

'Another milestone that will always stand out in the history of the squadron was the transition, while continuing to operate against the enemy, from P-47s to P-51s. Many of the crew chiefs and their assistants were crewing '47s and '51s at the same time. On 8 March, the squadron took off in two sections, one flying P-51s and the other flying P-47s.'

The group's mission that day was to escort the bombers as they returned from the attack on Berlin. An ominous cloud cover hung over England, possibly predicting the event that occurred shortly after the 486th FS departed from Bodney. The aircraft began lifting off of the runway at 1345 hrs, but tragedy struck before the mixed formation cleared the overcast. While trying to climb through the thick clouds, a mid-air collision took place and three P-47s crashed to earth, whilst a fourth made an emergency landing at a bomber base. One pilot from the 486th, Lt Earl Bond, was killed, and the others involved only avoided serious injury by either bailing out of their stricken Thunderbolts or by making an emergency landing.

The remainder of the 352nd continued on to its rendezvous point, arriving too late to participate in the heavy fighting that had taken place. The 352nd did, however, engage the enemy in two separate

Another member of the 486th FS's 'Snow White flight' was Lt Donald McKibben and his P-47D-15 (42-76323) named *SNEEZY*. This aircraft, coded 'PZ-Y', was destroyed on 8 March 1944 in a mid-air collision as his flight took off in zero visibility conditions at the start of a bomber escort mission to Berlin. Lt McKibben parachuted to safety (*Donald McKibben*)

Lt Al Wallace's brand new P-51B-5 43-7022 *Little Rebel* runs up at Bodney in early March 1944. The fighter participated in the 486th FS's history-making mission on the 8th of that month, when the group put up a split force of Mustangs and Thunderbolts. More significantly, this fighter was used by Capt Ed Gignac to down a Bf 109 during the course of this mission, thus registering the 352nd's first Mustang victory (*Al Wallace via Dwayne Tabatt*)

Another Messerschmitt fighter downed on 8 March was this Bf 109G-6 of German ace Hauptmann Klaus Mietusch, *Gruppenkommandeur* of III./JG 26. Having downed a B-17 earlier in the day to register his 60th kill, Mietusch succeeded in bailing out of his blazing fighter after becoming Capt Virgil Meroney's eighth victim (*Mrs Louise Meroney*)

encounters, and both were significant. The first occurred near Dümmer Lake, west of Hannover, when Capt Edward Gignac of the 486th FS observed a straggling B-17 being attacked by a Bf 109. He immediately went to its rescue, as he subsequently reported once back at Bodney;

'As I closed in on the '109 he broke off his attack on the bomber with what appeared to be a violent aileron roll, and then pulled up in a vertical climb. I reefed back violently and fired a short burst, but my closing speed was very high so I could not follow him up. Even though my burst was very short, and at great deflection, I claim destruction of this Me 109.'

Lt Ed Heller saw the German pilot bail out and confirmed the kill. Ed Gignac was flying P-51B-5 43-7022 'PZ-W', and his victory was the first of many that the 352nd FG would score with the Mustang.

The second kill of the mission was scored by Capt Virgil Meroney, who attacked the leader of three Bf 109s that were shooting up the bombers at the rear of the formation. The chase went from high altitude down to tree-top level and back up again, before Capt Meroney registered hits all over the fleeing Bf 109G-6. Moments later the aircraft burst into flames, and as it headed earthward its pilot, Hauptmann Klaus Mietusch, *Gruppenkommandeur* of III./JG 26, bailed out. Mietusch, who was injured whilst taking to his parachute, had earlier downed a B-17 that same day to raise his tally to 60 kills. The German ace would eventually be shot down and killed by future P-51 ace Lt William Beyer of the 361st FG on 17 September, having just claimed his 75th victory (a member of Beyer's flight) on what would be his 452nd, and last, combat sortie.

Having now scored his eighth victory, Virgil Meroney had firmly established himself as the 352nd's scoring leader. Indeed, his closest rival at this time was Don Bryan of the 328th with just 3.33 victories.

Two uneventful missions were flown on 9 March, but on the 11th the 352nd found itself in the thick of the action. The group was to fly a

Capt Virgil Meroney's P-47D-5 42-8473 *Sweet LOUISE* displays its pilot's final score of nine victories, the last of which was claimed on 16 March 1944. Also note the many broom symbols forward of the crosses, each one denoting a completed fighter sweep. All of Meroney's kills (and one damaged) were scored in this aircraft, as was George Preddy's second victory (*352nd FG Association*)

Crew Chief Albert F Giesting and Lt Meroney prepare *Sweet LOUISE* for another mission in February 1944. Meroney credited much of his success to the work of Sgt Giesting and his crew, this mutual respect later turning into a genuine friendship between the Meroney and Giesting families that has endured throughout the years (*Albert F Giesting*)

low-level sweep over the Pas de Calais to determine the strength of the German flak batteries in the area, and it proved to be a murderous assignment. Indeed, many surviving 'Bluenosers' consider it the most memorable, and dangerous, mission they ever flew.

The 36 aircraft involved started receiving ground fire when they were still three miles off the coast of France, and it intensified as they headed inland. None of the squadrons were able to strafe their assigned targets because of the thick and deadly flak, and virtually all of the P-47s taking part in the mission received some damage. Two pilots, Lts Harold Riley of the 487th and William Schwenke of the 328th were killed, and Lt Ralph Hamilton of the 487th was wounded.

11 March also saw another change of command in the 328th FS, when Pacific theatre five-kill ace Maj I B 'Jack' Donalson transferred in from the 487th FS (where he had been the squadron Operations Officer) to replace Harold Lund as CO.

The 352nd returned to bomber escort missions on 15 March, and added another five confirmed victories to its scoreboard. Four of the kills went to pilots of the 328th and the fifth was claimed by Capt Stephen Andrew of the 486th. Andrew had scored the first victory of the day when he destroyed a Bf 109 near Enschede, in Belgium, and after Henry Miklajcyk damaged a second Messerschmitt, the remaining enemy aircraft fled the area. Thirty minutes later the 328th spotted a gaggle of

Capt Virgil Meroney of the 487th FS was undoubtedly one of the best fighter pilots to serve with the 352nd FG in its early months in the ETO. Indeed, he was the group's only P-47 ace, and his score of aerial victories was more than double that of his closest rivals when he was shot down by flak in April 1944 (*via Sam Sox*)

14 Bf 109s and went into action. Two fell to Lt John Thornell, the third was claimed by Capt Don Bryan and the fourth Bf 109 was credited to Lt Fremont Miller.

The 'crew chief's side' of Capt Meroney's P-47 displays the names *Mrs Josephine* for Mrs Giesting and *Hedy* for Assistant Crew Chief Jack Gillenwater's wife (*Albert F Giesting*)

German fighters were again encountered on 16 March, and the 352nd notched up two more victories. The day's kills were scored by Lt Wendell Parlee of the 328th FS (his first) and Capt Virgil Meroney of the 487th. This proved to be the latter pilot's ninth, and last, kill, and the action took place over Bar-le-Duc, in France. A Bf 109 made a pass at Meroney's flight, and as the ace turned to meet the attack, the German made the fatal error of trying to out-dive a Thunderbolt. After being hit by a hail of gunfire, the burning Bf 109 attempted to loop away, but instead stalled 'off the top' and crashed.

During the remainder of March the 352nd flew eight more missions and claimed one additional victory. This came on the 23rd when Yellow Flight of the 328th FS, composed of Capt Earl Abbott and Lts John Thornell, Ed Zellner and Richard Brookins, bounced a He 177 near Hespe airfield and shot it down. The latter part of the month also saw yet another command change in the 328th FS when, on the 21st, Maj Willie O Jackson transferred in from the 486th FS, allowing Jack Donalson to return to the 487th FS as its Operations Officer.

The once mighty Luftwaffe had taken a terrible pounding during the course of March 1944, and now the Allied Air Forces effectively controlled the skies over Europe. Recognising that the Allies had indeed gained complete air superiority, *General der Jagdflieger* Adolf Galland moved his fighter units to bases deeper in Germany in an attempt to provide some sanctuary from attack. VIII Fighter Command alone had claimed the destruction of 406 aircraft in aerial combat and another 100 on the ground during March.

Because of this dramatic retreat by German fighter units, the average distance Allied pilots now had to fly before encountering enemy aircraft had increased to 350 miles. As a result, the P-47 groups rarely saw enemy fighters during early April due to the bulk of them being based beyond the Thunderbolt's range. The Luftwaffe also began hoarding its aircraft, sending them into action only if the odds were in their favour.

Faced with this situation, VIII Fighter Command was forced to change its tactics if it wanted to continue its destruction of the German air force. Senior officers therefore gave fighter groups the following

This view shows the 486th FS in transition in March 1944. In the foreground is Lt Earl Meyer's P-47D-5 42-8459 *"Bonnie Lee"*, coded 'PZ-E', whilst in the background is P-51B-5 43-6509 'PZ-H' assigned to Capt Chet Harker. The names *Cile II* and *THE LUCK OF THE IRISH* were later added to the Mustang (*352nd FG Association*)

An example of the 352nd's early light blue nose marking is illustrated on Lt Marion Nutter's P-51B-10 43-7160, *MARGIE*, coded 'HO-N'. The famous swept back blue nose soon replaced this marking. This aircraft was destroyed in a mid-air collision during a training sortie near Bodney on 18 June 1944. Its pilot, newly-arrived Lt Robert S Daugherty, was killed in the crash, having not yet flown an operational mission (*Sheldon Berlow*)

instruction – 'If they won't come up then find their bases and destroy them on the ground'. As this order was being fully digested, the 352nd was speeding up its conversion onto the Mustang.

During the first few days in April the 352nd continued flying missions with mixed formations of P-47s and P-51s. However, by the second week of the month the group had received enough Mustangs to fully equip both the 486th and 487th FSs. And along with the new fighters came the technical order which would soon provide the 352nd FG with its unique identity – the blue nose.

The fad of brightly coloured nose markings which began in the 56th FG in March 1944 quickly caught on with other fighter groups within the Eighth Air Force. VIII Fighter Command soon realised that the colourful markings provided an effective method of identifying a group in the air, and it immediately took steps to institute a standardised system. A secondary benefit of each group having its own unique markings was the positive effect it had on unit morale, better known as *esprit de corps*. This was particularly true within the 352nd FG.

Since the original complement of Mustangs received by the group had been a 'mixed bag' of both Olive Drab (OD) and natural metal machines, the blue paint initially adopted was light in shade so that it would still be noticeable on the OD P-51s. The original marking took the form of a blue spinner and a 12-inch band, or ring, around the nose, but by late April the distinctive swept-back 'bluenose' had made its first appearance.

On 8 April Col Joe Mason led his 'Bluenosers' into Germany on an escort mission, and after rendezvousing with two combat wings of the 3rd Bomb Division over Haaksbergan, in Holland, the group split up. The 328th, flying P-47s, escorted one formation of B-17s to Quackenbrück, and the 487th shepherded the other wing to Bramsche. The 486th FS, meanwhile, flew as top cover for both formations with its P-51s. As soon as the bombers had completed an extremely successful bomb run against the targets, the 328th dived down and ravaged Quackenbrück airfield with a series of punishing strafing attacks.

Before departing from the scene, the 328th had destroyed 12 aircraft, and five others were reported as probably destroyed. The sturdy P-47s brought their pilots home without a scratch, this mission proving to be a fitting 'swansong' for the Thunderbolts that were soon to be retired.

Many of the 486th and 487th FS pilots turned their guns toward locomotives and other targets of opportunity, but some individuals from the latter unit strafed Bramsche airfield, and this attack cost them the 352nd's leading ace, Capt Virgil Meroney. A chance hit by flak accomplished what the Luftwaffe's fighter pilots had been unable to do. He bailed out of his burning P-51 and landed safely after his 'chute opened at tree-top level. Meroney was soon captured, and spent the next year as a guest of the

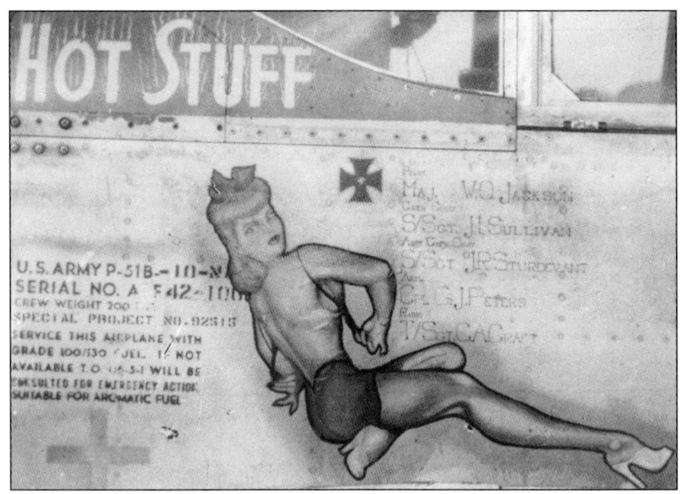

Maj Willie O Jackson's P-51B-10 42-106661 displayed a beautifully painted 'Vargas girl', appropriately named *Hot Stuff* (note the sizzling effect on the letters) below the cockpit. The solitary victory symbol on display here was credited to Jackson (flying his assigned P-47D-5 42-8452) on 20 February 1944. The seven-kill ace failed to make even a damaged claim in *Hot Stuff* before 'she' was shot down by flak near Le Merterault, in France, on 7 June 1944. Its pilot on this occasion was Maj Ed Gignac, who died in the crash (*Willie O Jackson*)

German government. He noted what had happened in his 'Kriegie Diary';

'After "bombs-away" our job with the bombers was through, so we dropped down to find some targets to shoot up. I spotted a JU-88 on one of the airdromes, and getting the go ahead from "J C", down I went with my Flight. I did okay. Set her on fire and saw very little flak to speak of. Took care of a few gun emplacements, buildings, etc. and got away all right. Soon picked up another airdrome that looked as if something should be on it. So down and after it.

'I didn't see anything on the first half of the field, but on the other side were several Me-410s. I was able to get only one on the first pass, but I got him burning good. Though there was plenty of groundfire, I came back around to try and get one more if possible. I got another burst into another '410 and it started to burn quickly. Then it happened! My engine on fire up to the firewall and both rudder pedals, and part of my left wing knocked off. She kept ticking over, though. A little hot for comfort, so back on the stick and a hope that I am high enough to bail out. Unable to see for the fire, so out I went, pulling the ripcord immediately. The 'chute opened at tree-top level, pretty close, and I hit the ground plenty hard!

'Out of my 'chute and a run for freedom, with the Germans firing at me all the time. I headed for some woods away from the Germans, but three more came out of the woods with guns drawn on me. My capture was made. Not much chance to get away, but I had tried. I spent the next two days at the fields I had strafed and saw what was left of the planes I hit before I was transferred to the *Dulag*.'

Virgil Meroney's P-51B-10 (43-7166 'HO-V') was the first Mustang to be lost in combat by the 352nd FG.

The group returned to Germany on 9 April, where it was greeted by a multitude of German fighters. The 328th FS initiated the action with an attack on three Fw 190s that were closing in on a formation of B-24s over Osnabrück. Lt Marion V Long blasted one of the Focke-Wulfs from the sky and Maj Willie O Jackson thoroughly worked over another fighter, reporting it as a probable. The third Fw 190 pilot then hastily left the area before he suffered the same fate. In another engagement over Osnabrück, the 328th FS's Lt Frederick Yochim was shot down and made a PoW.

After ensuring that the sky was clear of enemy fighters, the 486th and 487th FSs 'hit the deck' looking for targets of opportunity. The latter unit found Vechta airfield full of aircraft, torching 11 before moving on. Carl Luksic claimed three Ju 88s, and close behind him with two kills each were Capt Clayton Davis and Lts Clarence Palmer and Bill Whisner. However, the squadron's success was tempered by the death of Lt Ralph Williamson, whose Mustang inexplicably exploded off Harwich.

The 'Bluenosers' increased their tally of aircraft destroyed during a mission to France on 10 April. The action began when the 328th bounced some Fw 190s that were firing on the B-17s that the unit was escorting. Capt Donald Bryan and Lt Jamie Laing latched on to one of the Focke-Wulfs and shot it down. As their victim hit the ground, Lts John Thornell and Fremont Miller continued the assault on the Fw 190s, the latter hitting his target with a burst in the right wing that caused its landing gear to drop. At this point the pilot bailed out. John Thornell then shot up his prey, watching as the pilot also took to his parachute.

Capt Henry Miklajcyk (right) and his P-51B-10 42-106430 *The Syracusan*, coded 'PZ-K'. Miklajcyk scored heavily in this machine between 15 and 25 April, claiming two aerial victories and 4.5 strafing kills (five of these were scored on 24 April alone). Later to become a fully fledged aerial ace with 7.5 kills to his credit, Miklajcyk was killed in action on 2 November 1944 during an air battle over Merseburg, having just downed two German fighters (*352nd FG Association*)

Now it was the 487th's turn to engage the enemy, and the unit picked up from where the 328th had left off by downing four more fighters. Lt Robert O'Nan scored the first of the 487th's victories when he downed an Fw 190 near Rheims. Five minutes later Capt Clayton Davis and Lt Ernest McMahon shared a victory when their victim also crashed in a field outside of Rheims. The final two kills of the day were credited to John C Meyer and Carl Luksic, the first of these being an Fw 190 that they shared. Maj Meyer then chased a Bf 109 for 20 miles before sending it crashing into woodland.

Over the next several days the 'Bluenosers' carried out a series of destructive strafing attacks on airfields and other targets of opportunity. On the mission of 11 April the 486th and 487th FSs struck several airfields and destroyed 20 aircraft, probably destroyed two and damaged 17 – only two of the victories were aerial kills, scored by Lt Frank Cutler and Lt Woodrow Anderson of the 486th. After leaving the airfields, pilots of the 486th FS turned their attention to hunting down locomotives. One such strafing run cost the life of Lt Alfred Marshall, who was probably downed by debris from an exploding locomotive.

The 352nd continued its assault on German airfields on the 13th, with attacks on two sites near Stuttgart resulting in ten aircraft being destroyed and several more damaged. In the air, Lt Robert Ross of the 487th downed a biplane trainer which had blundered into the area. No 'Bluenosers' were lost, but the 486th's Lt Frank Cutler suffered a painful wound when a bullet came through the canopy and removed his left index finger.

Bill Kohlhas, Assistant Crew Chief of Maj John Meyer's *Lambie II*, takes a moment to pose with the scoreboard that his CO demanded be kept up to date. This photograph was taken in May 1944, when Meyer's tally of aerial victories stood at 8.5 and his strafing kills at 5.5. This particular aircraft (P-51B-10 42-106471) was lost on the same day as Willie O Jackson's *Hot Stuff*, 7 June 1944 (*William Kohlhas*)

On the return trip in his badly damaged Mustang, future 7.5-kill ace Cutler managed to apply a tourniquet while holding the stick between his knees. He next administered morphine, but for some reason his pain was not eased and he contemplated bailing out in order to get medical attention. In spite of the intense pain, Cutler stayed with his

P-51 and made an emergency landing at Woodbridge airfield two hours later.

Maj John C Meyer destroyed three of the day's total and raised his score to 9.5 (five of these were strafing kills). The combination of his new P-51B-10 *Lambie II* (42-106471) and the greater emphasis placed on strafing in April 1944 had enabled Meyer to nearly triple his score in less than a month. This rapid success led 'J C' Meyer to issue an urgent request to his groundcrew, which is related here by his assistant crew chief, Bill Kohlhas;

This P-51B-10, assigned to Lt Col Luther Richmond, did not last long enough to receive its blue nose paint job. When Richmond was shot down while strafing Vechta airfield on 15 April 1944, the fighter still carried its depot-applied OD spinner and nose band (*352nd FG Association*)

'Maj Meyer had just landed his P-51 after a victorious mission, and he told S/Sgt Conkey (crew chief) and me to get the aeroplane ready for the next mission, and be sure to get those new swastikas painted on. Knowing the amount of work required to prepare *Lambie II* for its next mission, Sgt Conkey's response was less than enthusiastic, and he stated "the swastikas were a low priority to him". Meyer's comeback was swift and to the point. "No Sgt Conkey, in my book it ranks high and here's why. On one of my early missions two German fighters covered in victory markings flew alongside me and looked me over – scared the hell out of me. Now that I have the opportunity to do the same, if I can't shoot them down, I'll scare them down". Needless to say, we damn well painted those swastikas onto his aeroplane.'

Lt Jack Thornell of the 328th FS poses for the press after his three-kill mission in his P-51B-15 42-106872 *Patty Ann II* ('PE-T') on 8 May 1944. Thornell would claim a total of nine kills in this particular Mustang (*John F Thornell*)

VIII Fighter Command was so pleased by the results of the strafing attacks during the first half of April 1944 that plans were prepared for a massive strafing mission on the 15th. On that day over 600 fighters of VIII and IX Fighter Commands would strike at airfields in central and western Germany, destroying 80 aircraft. Exactly half of these were shot down, with the remainder claimed on the ground. The cost of this success was high, however, for 19 Allied fighters were lost.

The 'Bluenosers' were one of the most successful units to participate in the mission, scoring seven aerial victories and one strafing kill for the loss of three aircraft and two pilots. The 486th FS saw its CO, Lt Col Luther Richmond, shot down in his new P-51B-10 (43-7196) by flak at Vechta, and he became a PoW. Lt Robert Ross of the 487th (flying with the 486th on this occasion) was not so lucky. His fighter, P-51B-10 43-7192, was hit by flak again near Vechta, and although he coaxed it out over the North Sea, the Mustang eventually crashed and Ross was killed. The final aircraft downed (and also the last Thunderbolt lost operationally by the 352nd) was P-47D-5 42-8511 of the 328th FS, flown by Lt Fremont Miller. His aircraft had been badly damaged when a building he was strafing at Vechta exploded, and he eventually bailed out over the Channel. Miller then spent the next 76 hours in a waterlogged dinghy until he was finally rescued. He never flew operationally with the 352nd again.

As this photograph clearly shows, Lt Don McKibben also took his nickname and painted lady with him to P-51B-10 42-106483 once he had transitioned from his P-47, featured on page 29. He is seen here (second from left) posing with his dedicated groundcrew (*Donald McKibben*)

The group next engaged enemy aircraft on 19 April, and it was an auspicious beginning for the 328th FS with the Mustang. Only two pilots from the squadron were on the mission, but they were the first to sight and attack the enemy fighters. The encounter took place south-west of Kassel when Lt John Thornell charged into a flight of seven Fw 190s and destroyed two of them, as well as damaging a third. With these kills Thornell raised his total to 6.25 kills to become the 352nd's second air-to-air ace. The third kill of the day was credited to Lt Donald McKibben of the 486th FS, who downed a Bf 109 in the vicinity of Kassel. The scoring continued the following day during a fighter sweep of France when pilots of the 486th and 487th claimed three more aerial victories.

Ground strafing then resumed in earnest, and during the missions of 22-24 April the 352nd destroyed 37 aircraft (one of which was an aerial victory) and damaged another 25. In addition to the aircraft destroyed, the 352nd was credited with the destruction of several other targets, including nine locomotives. The 328th suffered its first Mustang loss on the 22nd, however, when Lt Marion Long was downed by flak and became a PoW. Capt Robert McKean of the 486th was also lost to flak 48 hours later, although unlike Long he went in with his Mustang and was killed.

The group's stand-out strafing ace on 24 April was Lt Edwin Heller of the 486th FS, who destroyed seven aircraft and damaged five at Crailsheim-Bokingen airfield. This effort earned him the Distinguished Service Cross (DSC).

The group next tried its skill at dive-bombing when it attacked the airfield at Cormeilles-en-Vixen, in France, on 26 and 27 April. The results of the raids were rated only fair by VIII Fighter Command.

After these lacklustre missions, the 352nd returned to the more familiar role of bomber escort on the 28th.

Lt Ed Heller's P-51B-5 43-6704 *HELL-ER-BUST* was photographed 'in the field' at Bodney on a sunny day in May 1944. The Mustang displays ten German crosses along its cowling, the bulk of these being for strafing kills. Heller's fighter was one of the first Mustangs within the 352nd FG to be fitted with a Malcolm hood, and this was due primarily to the pilot's height (*Edwin L Heller*)

Maj Stephen Andrew of the 486th FS came to the 352nd FG having already seen action in the Pacific. Indeed, he had a Zero kill to his credit, hence the rising sun marking alongside the five crosses on his P-51B-10 42-106467 ('PZ-A'). Having claimed nine aerial kills and 6.5 strafing victories by 30 May 1944, Andrew became a PoW after this very aircraft suffered an engine failure over Budapest on 2 July 1944 (*Sheldon Berlow*)

The blue nose on Al Wallace's *Little Rebel* (seen without this marking on page 30) appears to be a shade lighter than standard, perhaps to provide a better contrast against its OD paint scheme (*352nd FG Association via Marc Hamel*)

After the bombers had completed their runs over Avord and Herbeville airfields, the 328th FS headed down to strafe the targets that had just been bombed. Herbeville was attacked first, and Lt Robert Powell managed to set fire to a Ju 88 parked in a hangar before his aircraft took damaging hits in the tail section and his wingman, Lt Jamie Laing, was shot down. Laing survived bailing out to become a PoW.

The 328th then turned its attention to Avord, where Capt Robert Sharpe and Lt Powell shared in the destruction of another Ju 88. The 486th and 487th also struck at other airfields in the area, destroying six aircraft. Lt Fred Allison of the 487th led the scoring with two victories.

During the next two missions the 352nd added another five aerial and two strafing victories to its scoreboard. One of these kills stands out for providing a moment of sheer horror for the pilots of the 486th FS. The engagement, which occurred on 30 April, began ordinarily enough, with the Fw 190 pilot taking evasive action in an attempt to shake Capt Stephen Andrew off of his tail. As the P-51 pilot closed on his prey, the macabre sequence of events began. Capt Andrew's report tells the story;

'On resuming the chase I closed to 200 yards and less and opened fire. I did a pretty sloppy job of shooting – I was deflecting and shooting off-line. There had been a party the night before which I blame for that. However, I did get a few strikes, and I think I damaged his engine because he seemed to suddenly lose power. That caused me to overshoot, and I found myself flying in tight formation with him on his left wing.

'The enemy pilot had his head down as if he was checking his instruments. I noticed that the elastic band on his goggles was white. He raised his head and saw me – I would have waved if he had given me the chance, but he peeled away and I re-opened fire from very close range. This time he jettisoned his canopy and stood up in the cockpit. When he bailed out he was swept directly into the hub of my prop. I was too close to avoid him. There was quite a violent jar and my engine ran rough, so I called my flight around me and set course for home.

'An examination after landing revealed considerable damage to the spinner and prop. There was a slight dent in the port wing root, and there were bits of flesh in the air ducts, and a small piece of bone stuck in one blade of the prop. A piece of the enemy pilot's blue coveralls, about six inches square, was stuck on the bolt that helps hold the spinner on. I put it away to remember him by.

'My flight gave me excellent support during the engagement, and I genuinely appreciated their presence during our return.'

April had also seen two more command changes within the group, with Maj Willie O Jackson returning to the 486th from the 328th FS on the 19th to replace Lt Col Luther Richmond as CO – the latter had been shot down on 15 April. Back at the 328th, Maj Hal Lund once again took command of the unit.

As April 1944 passed into history, it was quite obvious that VIII Fighter Command's aggressive new tactics had paid off. During the month its pilots had claimed 825 aircraft destroyed, of which 493 were classified as strafing kills. The 352nd was credited with 138 of those victories, 33 of which came in aerial combat. The cost was not insignificant, however, with VIII Fighter Command losing 163 aircraft, ten of them 'Bluenosers'.

Maj George Preddy and his crew chief Lew Lunn pose with their P-51B-10 42-106451 *Cripes A'Mighty* after the former's double victory on 22 April 1944. Recently discovered photographs show that the name was not followed by '2nd' as previously believed. This aircraft, was lost on 16 July 1944 with Jule V Conard at the controls, the fighter having suffered mechanical failure over Munich. The pilot survived to become a PoW (*Sheldon Berlow*)

George Preddy (sat in an OD Mustang) quizzes fellow pilots on their success in a recent mission in this heavily posed shot taken in the spring of 1944. Standing on the fighter's starboard wing is Lt Malcolm C Pickering, who claimed four aerial and four strafing victories. At the extreme left of the photo is Lt Jack Thornell, who claimed 17.25 aerial kills to finish third in the group's post-war ace listing – he was, however, the ranking ace of the 328th FS (*via Michael O'Leary*)

Lt John Bennett's P-51B-5 43-6506 had the distinction of being one of only a handful of sharkmouthed Mustangs to serve with VIII Fighter Command. Assigned to the 487th FS, the fighter received its ferocious nose-art in the early spring of 1944 (*via Sam Sox*)

PRELUDE TO D-DAY

Early May 1944 saw more changes in Eighth Air Force operations now that aerial superiority had been achieved. Gen Dwight Eisenhower and his staff tasked both the Eighth and Ninth Air Forces in England with the job of clearing the way for the impending invasion of Occupied Europe. To help achieve these goals, the Eighth diverted its bomber and fighter units from targets deep in Germany to tactical targets in France and Belgium during the first few days of the month.

The 352nd FG participated in a number of these tactical missions in the opening week of May, although they proved to be uneventful. On the 7th the group returned to its bomber escort duties, flying its first mission to Berlin. Enemy aircraft were conspicuous by their absence that day, but the mission of 8 May would be a totally different story.

The targets were Berlin and Brunswick, and this time the air was filled with well over 200 German fighters. Indeed, when the 'Bluenosers' arrived over Brunswick there was no need to search out enemy aircraft because they were swarming throughout the patrol area allocated to the 352nd FG. Dogfights began almost immediately, and in a series of engagements that lasted nearly an hour, the 'Bluenosers' claimed a total of 27 destroyed, two probably destroyed and six damaged.

It was a day of multiple victories by individual pilots, and Lt Carl Luksic of the 487th FS proved to be the day's top scorer with five kills (he had claimed two aerial victories and a handful of strafing kills prior to this sortie). This feat gave him the distinction of being the Eighth Air Force's first 'ace in a day'. His encounter report gives an accurate description of the action;

'While he (Lt Bob O'Nan) was chasing this '109 I saw on my left five or six FW 190s which I immediately turned into. Lt O'Nan at this time was engaged with the '109. I put down ten degrees of flaps and started queuing up on one of the '190s. I fired very short bursts from about 300 yards, 15 degrees deflection and observed many strikes on the canopy and fuselage. He immediately pulled up and rolled over and the pilot

A pleased looking 1Lt Carl Luksic of the 487th FS illustrates how many German fighters he downed on the escort mission to Brunswick on the morning of 8 May 1944. The first Eighth Air Force pilot to become an 'ace in a day', Luksic was awarded a DSC for his efforts. A total of 19 pilots would achieve this unique feat with VIII Fighter Command during World War 2, four of whom came from the 352nd FG. The only other USAAF group to boast so many 'aces in a day' was the P-47-equipped 56th FG (*352nd FG Association*)

Maj Edward Gignac's P-51B-10, and its groundcrew (Art Nellen on the wing and Cy Hall standing), are seen at Bodney in May 1944. Following Gignac's death on 7 June in P-51B-10 42-106661, this aircraft was assigned to other pilots within the 486th. One of the last B-models to serve with the group, it was finally written off following Joe Shaw's fiery crash-landing in early 1945 (*Cyrus Hall via Marc Hamel*)

bailed out, the aeroplane going straight in from 1500 ft. Capt Cutler, 486th Squadron, saw this one take place.

'At this time in this vicinity there were three 'chutes – one from the enemy aircraft that I had shot down and one from the enemy aircraft that Lt O'Nan had shot down, but I do not know where the third one came from.

'I then broke away from one shooting at me and got onto another '190's tail and fired short bursts, but did not see any hits. However, the pilot evidently spun out as he went straight into the ground from 800 ft or so and blew up. I was then joined by two P-47s but lost them, and finally joined up with two from our own group, namely Capt Cutler and his wingman. He started down over Brunswick to strafe a drome, but observing so much ground fire and flak I pulled up and away and lost them.

'I then saw another aeroplane which I thought to be a P-51. I closed on it to about 25 to 30 yards and identified it as a '109. I gave a short burst, but don't know if there were any strikes, and I found myself riding his wing as I was at full throttle. He was about 200 ft off the deck, and when he looked at me he pulled up, jettisoned his canopy and bailed out. I went down and took a picture of the aeroplane, which had crashed into a small wood, and right onto a small fire.

'I then started to climb back up when I was rejoined by my wingman, Lt O'Nan, and Red Leader, Capt Davis. We started back towards the bombers when off to our left at nine o'clock low we observed about 20 to 25 Me-109s in close formation going down through the clouds. The three of us immediately turned into the attack and came down on them through the clouds. I found myself directly astern of a '190, with a '109 flying his wing in close formation. I was evidently unseen as I got in a very successful burst at the '109 and observed numerous hits on his wings, fuselage and tail. He was at about 800 to 1000 ft, and after catching fire he went straight down into the ground.

'I immediately kicked a little right rudder and got in another successful burst at the '190 and observed numerous hits on its left wing, engine

This photograph shows Lt Col John Meyer's *Lambie II* as it looked in May 1944, just before its pilot went home on 30 days leave. Although it displays 18 Iron Crosses below the cockpit, Meyer's actual score at the time stood at 15.5 kills (both aerial and ground kills). The additional crosses must have represented enemy aircraft that he had claimed as probably destroyed or damaged (*352nd FG Association*)

This close up of 'J C' and *Lambie II* reveals just how tight a fit the cockpit of the early P-51B was for pilots of bigger than average build (*via Sam Sox*)

and canopy. The '190 went into a tight spiral and crashed into the deck from 1000 ft.

'At this point there were about 15 or more enemy aircraft in the vicinity and they started aggressive tactics, and since I was alone, and they were making head-on passes at me, I had to take violent evasive action. I evaded into the clouds.'

With these five victories Lt Carl Luksic raised his total score to eight. Following close behind Luksic that day were John C Meyer, John Thornell and Clayton Davis with three victories each. One tense moment occurred for Jack Thornell when he was bounced by an aggressive Bf 109. Thinking that he was out of ammunition when the Messerschmitt jumped him, Thornell radioed for help.

While awaiting assistance, he succeeded in outmanoeuvring the Bf 109 and now found himself on its tail. John C Meyer, instead of coming to the rescue, called out for Thornell to 'chew his tail off – you are close enough'.

Lt Thornell, less than pleased with this type of help, turned inside the Bf 109 and closed to within 10-15 yards of it. The German pilot, thinking he was about to be rammed, quickly bailed out. Col Mason overhead the radio chatter between Meyer and Thornell and was extremely upset with Meyer's 'assistance'. After the group returned to base Col Mason laid down the law in no uncertain terms that his pilots would not ram an enemy aeroplane!

The 352nd suffered one combat loss on 8 May when the 487th's

Lt George Kopecy was shot down over Nienburg by German fighters – he became a PoW. The 486th also lost Lt John Worchester on this day when he crashed his P-51 whilst training 352nd FG pilots how to dive-bomb.

The historic action of 8 May 1944 earned the 352nd FG the Distinguished Unit Citation, and a number of its pilots were also awarded DSCs for their individual actions.

Following a detour to targets in France on the 9th, the 'Bluenosers' returned to Germany on 12 May. This mission would usher in one of the most productive periods of the war for the 352nd FG. In the vicinity of Prenzlau, in Germany, John Meyer observed a combat wing of B-17s being rocked by explosions throughout the formation, and he led eight 487th Mustangs down to investigate.

As the fighters approached the Fortresses, several parachutes were seen in the air, and then Meyer spied the large formations of enemy aircraft. The first two gaggles that he spotted were quickly lost in the heavy haze, but one Bf 109 in the third flight was not so lucky. He failed to reach the sanctuary offered by the haze quickly enough, and Lt Col Meyer set the fighter ablaze with one burst. After watching the Bf 109 crash, 'J C' made a strafing run across an airfield and destroyed a He 177, raising his total score to 15.5 (8.5 of which were aerial kills).

These victories came close to being his last when a Bf 109 bounced Meyer as he pulled up from his strafing run. The German was finally evaded after a series of violent manoeuvres, and John Meyer headed home from what would be his last mission of his first tour of duty.

Lt Fred Allison also had a very productive day by destroying 2.5 aircraft. Upon his arrival south-west of Koblenz with the rest of Red Flight, he observed an airfield below him and led his flight down to strafe it. He caught his first victim on the runway and set it on fire after a couple of bursts from his 'fifties', and then as Lt Allison pulled up he engaged another Bf 109 at about 200 ft and shared this kill with Lt Robert Butler.

After despatching this Bf 109 Allison had just turned in order to make another strafing run when he spotted another Messerschmitt fighter at an altitude of just 100 ft. His first burst of fire at the German fighter

Lt Fred Allison's P-51B-10 *Opal LEE* sits awaiting its next mission in May 1944. One of the 487th FS's original cadre of pilots upon the squadron's establishment (as the 34th FS) in late 1942, Allison served with the unit until declared tour-expired in June 1944. By then he had completed 70 missions and 202 hours of combat flying, claiming 1.5 aerial and two strafing victories (*Fred Allison*)

apparently panicked its pilot to the point that he put his aircraft into a dive and hit the ground in a fiery explosion. Red Flight's final victory of the day was scored by Lt David McEntire, who downed a low-flying Bf 109 near Koblenz airfield.

Four other victories were also claimed on the mission, three of which were aerial kills scored by Maj Stephen Andrew of the 486th FS, Lt Col Eugene Clark of the 328th FS (both one apiece) and Lts John Galiga of the 328th and Lt Harry Barnes of the 487th FS (one shared). The final victory of the day was a Ju 52 destroyed on the ground by Lt Bill Whisner of the 487th FS. The 352nd FG's overall tally for the 12th was ten destroyed and two damaged at the cost of one of its own – Lt Alfred F Howard of the 487th was killed when he was downed by German fighters.

Lt Bill Whisner and his P-51B-10 42-106449 pose for a PR shot after a successful mission on 12 May 1944. By 30 May the future ace had been credited with 3.5 aerial victories and three strafing victories. The fighter's unique nickname came about when a senior Eighth Air Force press officer suggested to Whisner's CO, Lt Col Meyer, that a suitably named Mustang might impress the future Queen of England during her impending visit to Bodney in May 1944. The only unnamed bare metal machine in the squadron at the time was 42-106449, and it was duly decorated with the name *Princess ELIZABETH*. Whisner was unaware of this until after the artwork had been applied, and he was not best pleased either with the nickname or the attendant press publicity! (*352nd FG Association*)

The aerial battles of 12 May had cost the Luftwaffe 61 fighters destroyed, and the slaughter continued the following day. On that date Allied fighter pilots would claim a further 58 aerial victories, 16 of which were credited to the 'Bluenosers'. The 352nd's big day, however, was not without dissension and tragedy for the 486th FS.

As the 352nd FG arrived at its rendezvous point, the Ninth Air Force's P-47-equipped 356th FG was already fighting off German attacks. While that engagement continued, the 'Bluenosers' escorted the bombers on to the target area without further incident. If any of the pilots were beginning to believe the remainder of the mission was going to be a 'milk run', however, this illusion was quickly brought to an end when they neared Tribsees-Demmin. Here, they encountered huge formations of German fighters, and a series of dogfights began.

The air battles continued for 30 minutes, Blue Flight of the 328th FS making the initial contact, and drawing first blood. Capt John Coleman and Lt Francis Horne each downed two enemy aircraft in the brief encounter – these kills gave the latter pilot (aerial) ace status. The unusual aspect of Coleman's victories was that he reported his victims as 'Me 109Es', despite this variant having been pulled from frontline service in Western Europe in 1941!

The 328th's Capt Earl Abbott and his groundcrew with *Flossie II*, alias P-51B-15 42-106844 'PE-A' (*352nd FG Association*)

Now it was the 486th's turn to engage the enemy, and its quarry was a force of at least 100 fighters. Col Joe Mason ordered the bounce, leading White Flight through the middle of the German formation in an attempt to break it up. As White Flight passed through their midst, the enemy aircraft did indeed split up, with some of them diving away and others climbing.

Red Leader, Capt Franklyn Greene, followed two of the diving Bf 109s down to 1500 ft and destroyed one of them. Lt Stan Miles, Red 3, started after another Messerschmitt, and as he did so his Mustang was hit in the left stabiliser by a German drop tank released from above. Ignoring the damage, Miles continued after the Bf 109 and shot it down before nursing his crippled P-51 back to Bodney.

Yellow Leader, Capt Woodrow Anderson, chased one of the Bf 109s that had begun to climb, and after stalking it through the clouds for several minutes, he shot it down in flames. Anderson also reported the enemy aircraft as an 'Me 109E'.

Strafing ace Lt Don Whinnem of the 486th FS used his P-51B-15 42-106752 *H.M.S. HELLION* ('PZ-W') to great effect during the spring and summer of 1944. A participant in the Russian 'Shuttle Mission' of 21 June, he downed a Bf 109 with this machine en route to the USSR. Whinnem later added a probable and a damaged to his totals in 42-106752 on 5 August 1944, as well as five strafing kills (and six probably destroyed on the ground) during his ETO tour. Whinnem left the 486th in September 1944, whereupon his aircraft was assigned to other pilots and eventually renamed *Little Ann* (*352nd FG Association*)

Meanwhile, Joe Mason was firing at Bf 109s he encountered while breaking up the German formation, and he later reported;

'I saw strikes on the wing of one Me-109. Upon coming out on the far side, I lost the rest of my flight. As I pulled up in a climbing turn and looked down at the large formation of bandits, I saw two Me-109s spinning down, one with about two-thirds of its wing gone. This collision was forced by my flight flying through the large formation of bandits at about a 90-degree angle. I am not certain as to whether the '109 I damaged was one of the two I later saw going down.

'My wingman broke away and down when we started through, and my second element pulled up and came in on the rear of the bandits. They did not see the collision. I then rolled back and down, chasing 15 to 20 FW 190s and Me-109s which had split off from the bunch and were diving for the clouds. I closed on an FW 190 and after a few short bursts, set him on fire. The first burst knocked his left flap off, or some object of similar size. He was taking evasive action in the clouds, and just before entering one, smoke, flame and debris came back over my ship and we both went into the cloud. I then pulled up to keep from running into him in the cloud, and came out on top. My ship was covered with oil from the '190. I claim two Me-109s and one Fw 190 destroyed, one Me-109 damaged.'

Joe Mason's victory over the Fw 190 was not questioned, but his claim for the two Bf 109s was not well received by the rest of his flight. They felt if credit was to be given it should have been shared equally by all pilots in White Flight. Mason was nevertheless credited with all three kills, taking his aerial tally to exactly five victories.

During the overall confusion of this fiercely contested action, 7.5-victory ace Capt Frank Cutler was killed when his P-51 collided with a Bf 109. The only eyewitness to the event was Lt Marion Nutter of the 487th FS, who saw Cutler (widely regarded by his contemporaries as one of the most aggressive pilots in the group) closing fast on the Bf 109;

'Suddenly a burst of flame appeared and both friendly and enemy aircraft seemed to fuse together. The P-51 apparently ran into the tail of the '109. I saw no explosion, nor did I see either of the pilots bail out.'

Col Joe Mason, CO of the 352nd FG, and Capt Frank Cutler of the 486th FS pose for the camera during late April 1944. Both became aces in May, and Cutler was killed when he collided with a Bf 109 on the 13th of that month – the very day Mason 'made ace' (*352nd FG Association*)

P-51C-1 43-103320 'HO-M' was the assigned aircraft of two of the 487th FS's most successful pilots, namely Lts Glennon Moran and Ray Littge. Initially flown by 'Bubbles' Moran, he used the fighter to score the majority of his 13 aerial and three strafing victories. This photograph was taken in August 1944, as evidenced by Moran's complete score displayed on the fuselage. After he left the squadron in August 1944, 43-103320 was assigned to Ray Littge, who later claimed 10.5 aerial and 13 ground kills (*Air Force Museum*)

The 486th's last kill of the day was a Bf 109 downed by Capt Donald Higgins.

At this point the 487th FS joined in the fight, and increased the 352nd's tally by four. George Preddy led the bounce on a flight of approximately 30 Bf 109s, and personally downed two of them – he had now achieved ace status, these kills taking his tally to 5.333 aerial victories. As the remaining Bf 109s tried to flee from the area Lt Nutter closed in and sent another fighter down in flames. The day's action was closed by a shared victory, Lts Carl Luksic and Glennon Moran interrupting a lone Ju 88 attacking a B-17. In a one-sided fight, they quickly forced the twin-engined interceptor to crash-land in a ploughed field. Observing that the Junkers twin had not caught fire after its landing, Luksic went down and strafed it. When he and Moran left the scene the Ju 88 was ablaze.

With 16 aerial victories to its credit, the 352nd FG was VIII Fighter Command's top scoring unit on 13 May, and Col Joe Mason was awarded the DSC for the part he played in the mission.

Following an 11-day lull in attacks on Berlin and Brunswick, the Eighth Air Force hit both cities again on 19 May. Berlin was the primary target, and nearly 600 B-17s headed for the German capital, while a secondary force of 390 B-24s set a course for Brunswick. Escort was provided by 14 Eighth Air Force fighter groups, supported by five from the Ninth Air Force's IX Fighter Command.

The Luftwaffe, as expected, was up in force to meet the massive American armada, and air battles occurred throughout the duration of the mission. By the end of it, pilots of VIII Fighter Command had claimed a total of 70 aerial victories, with a further 20 aircraft destroyed and 18 damaged on the ground. Ninth Air Force pilots chipped in with an additional four aerial kills

P-51B-10 43-7174 *The Duchess V* was flown by Lt Dick Brookins of the 328th FS. He scored 1.5 of his 4.25 aerial victories in this fighter, which was coded 'PE-I'. 43-7174 was lost in an operational accident on 9 June 1944, its pilot, Capt Robert Sharp, being killed (*352nd FG Association*)

Although the original print for this photo is at a crazy angle, it nevertheless gives a good close-up of the artwork carried by Capt Henry White's P-51B-5 43-6934 *Dallas Darling* (coded 'PE-H'). Note the natural metal framing of the canopy (a replacement item perhaps) on this otherwise OD Mustang. Capt White downed an Fw 190 in this aircraft on 28 May – one of two aerial victories he would claim during his 89-mission tour of the ETO that lasted until VE-Day (*352nd FG Association*)

Lt Ed Zellner of the 328th FS poses in his P-51B-15 42-106832 *We Three* at Bodney in May 1944. He had claimed 3.25 aerial victories and two strafing kills by the time he was shot down by flak (on his 89th mission) on 31 July 1944. Zellner successfully evaded capture (*Ed Zellner*)

and thirteen strafing victories. These scores had been achieved at a high price, however, for the USAAF lost 20 fighters and 28 bombers.

The 352nd was right in the thick of the action, being officially credited with 7.5 destroyed, two probably destroyed and two damaged for the loss of Lt Michael Carlone of the 328th. He had just finished off a Bf 109 that had been damaged by Capt Robert Sharp when his Mustang snap-rolled into trees moments after he attempted to pull up.

Carlone had almost certainly fallen victim to a sudden change in the fighter's centre of gravity, brought on by the movement of fuel in the aircraft's fuselage tank when he attempted a high-G pull out. Pilots were warned of this deadly trait, which affected only those Mustangs that had an additional fuselage tank fitted. The only way to eliminate this problem was to burn off as much fuel from this tank as possible before attempting high-G turns.

With the planned invasion of Europe drawing closer, the Eighth Air Force turned its attention to the German rail and transportation systems on 21 May. These attacks were appropriately called 'Chattanooga', and each fighter group would patrol the same areas that they had been assigned for airfield strafing. A total of 552 fighters from VIII Fighter Command swooped down and devastated all kinds of targets throughout Germany. The rail system, in particular, was dealt a punishing blow, losing 91 locomotives and having a further 134 damaged. Trucks, staff cars and airfields also received the same treatment. In addition to the destruction on the ground, US fighters claimed 20 aerial kills and 100 strafing victories.

The 352nd's day was quite successful, with the group claiming 20 aircraft destroyed and 13 damaged on the ground, as well as ten locomotives destroyed and numerous other rail and ground targets damaged. The 328th FS accounted for all of the aircraft, with Lt Ray Phillips leading the way with three destroyed. Lt Robert H 'Punchy' Powell Jr ran him a close second with two destroyed and two damaged. The most unusual report of the day was filed by Lt Ed Zellner, who destroyed 25 enemy cows!

Many other claims were made by the 486th and 487th FSs, including locomotives, a river steamer and numerous rail cars. During these attacks, Lt Col Eugene Clark of the HQ flight was downed by flak and crash-landed in a ploughed field. He was quickly picked up and spent the rest of the war as a PoW.

Another 'Chattanooga' was flown on 22 May, and White Flight of the 486th made the only claims – two locomotives destroyed and one damaged. The 'Chattanooga' sorties were followed up by a couple of tactical missions in France, one of which saw the group try its hand at 'bridge-busting'. However, as with its previous attempt at dive-bombing, this mission was not very successful. No losses were suffered, which was of some consolation, for earlier in May two of the group's pilots (Lt John B Worchester of the

The first Mustang assigned to future 13-kill ace Lt Glennon Moran had a very short life span, as this photograph clearly shows. Note how the ventral air intake has been completely ripped away, leaving a gaping hole in the underfuselage of P-51B-5 43-6912. The fighter's Hamilton Standard propeller has also taken a battering in the belly landing. The fighter was subsequently stripped of all serviceable components and scrapped (*352nd FG Association*)

Notice anything unusual about this photo of Jack Thornell's *PATTY ANN II*? Crew chief S/Sgt G A McIndoo added two extra gun ports to 'their' four-gun P-51B through the subtle use of paint! (*352nd FG Association*)

486th on 8 May and Capt Ernest B McMahan of the 487th the following day) had been killed in crashes whilst practising dive-bombing.

The 'Bluenosers' returned to escort duty on 24 May, shepherding bombers of the 3rd Task Force to Berlin. As they arrived in the target area numerous enemy aircraft were in evidence, and the 352nd joined the action. Red Flight of the 328th struck first, and Lts Ed Zellner and Bill Furr each downed a Bf 109. Things then quietened down for 30 minutes, before the 486th ran into another flight of aircraft, and Capt Woodrow Anderson and Lt Joe Gerst sent two more Messerschmitts down in flames.

While these encounters were taking place, the 487th FS searched for targets on the ground, and 17 locomotives were destroyed. However, the unit had 8.5-kill ace Lt Carl Luksic and newly-arrived replacement pilot Lt James Hannon both shot down by flak and made PoWs.

Three days later, on 27 May, Lt Col John Edwards led the 352nd on an escort mission, taking the group to north-eastern Germany. As the formation passed through France it ran into a large force of between 75 and 100 enemy aircraft between Épinal and Strasbourg. The German fighters were aggressively attacking the bombers, and Edwards led his force of 24 Mustangs into action. For the next 30 minutes the 'Bluenosers' were engaged in a series of classic dogfights, and when it was all over 13 enemy aircraft had been shot down.

Three aces scored kills on this occasion, the 328th's Lt John Thornell claiming two Bf 109s to take his aerial tally to 11.25 kills, Lt Glenn Moran also getting a brace of fighters to boost his score to 4.5 aerial kills and Capt Walter Starck being credited with a solitary Bf 109 to double his tally to date. The latter pilots were both from the 487th FS.

Even with the overwhelming strength of the Allied Air Forces, the Luftwaffe was still able to occasionally strike a punishing blow against the 'heavies', and this is exactly what happened on 28 May when the bombers struck oil refineries and aircraft factories in central Germany. Over 400 single- and 50 twin-engined fighters were waiting for the bomber stream in the Magdeburg area. The German tactic was to separate the escorts from the bombers, and while a portion of the enemy fighters kept USAAF fighters busy, the remaining Luftwaffe interceptors hit the bombers. The tactic worked well that day, for 17 bombers and 27 fighters were lost. It was also a costly day for the Luftwaffe, as 50 of its fighters fell to US guns.

The 352nd FG accounted for seven of the enemy aircraft destroyed on the 28th, and lost one of its own in the battle – 486th FS ace Capt Woodrow Anderson, who had claimed 4.5 aerial kills and nine strafing victories. His three-aeroplane flight had been bounced by 25 fighters, and sometime during the dogfight Anderson was shot down just after scoring his last aerial kill. Walter Starck saw him bail out, but his 'chute did not open.

The other two pilots in Anderson's flight fought their way out of the German bounce, claiming 2.5 Bf 109s destroyed in the process. Lt Ed Heller was credited with one and one shared (the latter with Lt Joe Lang of the 4th FG), while Lt Lester Howell claimed the other Messerschmitt. The remaining kills of the day were credited to Capt Stephen Andrew (his eighth victory) of the 486th, Lts Henry White of the 328th and Lt Harry Barnes of the 487th.

VIII Bomber Command again targeted aircraft production facilities and the petroleum industry on 29 May, attacking nine primary targets in eastern Germany. Overall, the Luftwaffe's reaction to these attacks was generally weak, but that was not true in the zone patrolled by the 352nd.

In separate actions involving the 487th and the 328th FSs, the 'Bluenosers' claimed another seven confirmed kills. One of these was particularly significant, for the German pilot had been observed attacking helpless Americans as they floated down in parachutes. Lts Glennon Moran and Jule Conard were incensed by what they saw and went after the Bf 109. The German observed them coming and tried to evade, but to no avail. Moran was finally able to get him in his sights and damage the fighter's tail section before Lt Conard finished the job.

The 352nd closed out its scoring for May 1944 with 14.5 victories on the 30th. On that date the 'Bluenosers' escorted bombers of the 1st Air Division to central Germany, where they found themselves engaged in a major battle over the target area. A force of 300+ enemy fighters opposed the USAAF formation, and they managed to down 13 bombers, but at a cost of nearly 60 of their own aircraft.

The initial skirmish took place near Halberstadt when Lts Bill Furr

P-51C-5 42-103341 *Spirit of Lufbery* ('HO-C') was assigned to Lt Jule V Conard of the 487th FS, who scored 0.5 of his 2.5 aerial victories in this aircraft. Conard was lost on 16 July 1944 when his Mustang (George Preddy's P-51B *Cripes A'Mighty*) suffered a mechanical failure over Munich, forcing him to bail out near the German town of Aalen. Conard survived to become a PoW (*352nd FG Association*)

A poor quality photo, but a rare one. This is the only known shot showing a full view of Lt Robert Frascotti's ill-fated P-51B-5 43-6685 *Umbriago*, circa April 1944. The pilot died in this aircraft when he flew into a newly-built control tower at Bodney during his take-off run in the pre-dawn darkness of D-Day morning (*352nd FG Association*)

A good 'photo in time'. Note that invasion stripes have been applied to the wings, but not as yet to the fuselage, of P-51B-10 42-106472 *The FLYING SCOT II* – coded 'PZ-D dot', the 'dot' being visible behind the lowered flaps. When the 'D' was relocated to the fighter's nose following the addition of the stripes, the dot came with it. The P-51's original pilot was 'Scottie' Cunningham, and when he returned to the US in early June it was assigned to Lt 'Bud' Fuhrman, who flew it on the 'Shuttle' mission to Russia (*352nd FG Association*)

and Richard Brookins of the 328th FS saw a mixed flight of Bf 109s and Fw 190s below them and attacked. Furr chased a Focke-Wulf from 20,000 ft down to the deck, where he fired just one burst and its pilot bailed out. As he pulled up he found himself behind another enemy fighter, so he latched onto it. An unidentified P-51 also joined in the chase, and as they closed on the Fw 190, the pilot jumped. This time not a shot had been fired!

Lt Brookins, meanwhile, had also scored an economical kill by chasing a Bf 109 in a steep dive. Firing only 40 rounds at his foe, Brookins watched as the fighter failed to recover from its dive and crashed.

High above this action the 486th and 487th FSs waded into another formation of aircraft, and in a 15-minute battle destroyed seven more German fighters and claimed an eighth as a probable. In contrast to these rough and tumble dogfights, Maj George Preddy and Lt Bill Whisner shared three Bf 109s as easily as shooting ducks in a shooting gallery.

They had witnessed a gaggle of 20+ Bf 109s attacking a formation of bombers and slipped in behind them. Preddy had downed two of the Messerschmitts before the German pilots realised that they were under attack, and as he and Whisner turned toward the next Bf 109, its pilot tried to evade the bounce but was too slow. Preddy crippled the fighter before running out of ammunition, leaving Whisner to finish it off.

Fifteen minutes later Lt Robert Berkshire of the 487th pulled off the same trick when he downed a Bf 109 before its pilot even realised he was in danger. He followed this up with his second kill of the mission (taking his final aerial tally to 4.5 kills) a little while later. Glennon Moran then completed the day's scoring with yet another double haul.

This highly successful mission closed out a fantastic two-month scoring spree for the 352nd FG. During April and May the 'Bluenosers' had destroyed 271 aircraft, probably destroyed 15 and damaged 86 in aerial combat or ground strafing. Literally hundreds of ground targets (trains, trucks and ships) had also been attacked, as had numerous other targets of opportunity. During this same period 17 'Bluenosers' were lost in combat operations and several others in accidents.

COLOUR PLATES

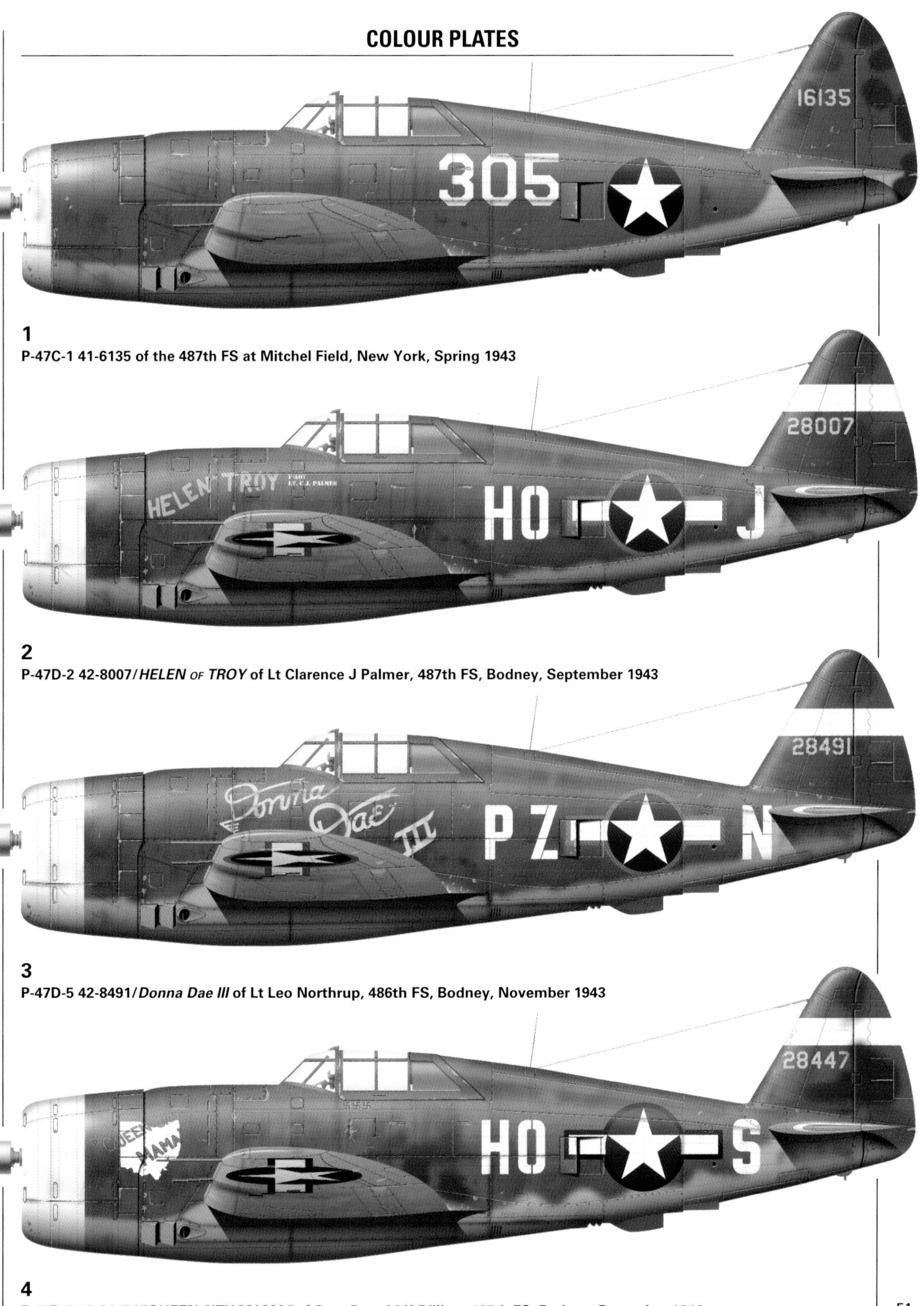

1
P-47C-1 41-6135 of the 487th FS at Mitchel Field, New York, Spring 1943

2
P-47D-2 42-8007/*HELEN OF TROY* of Lt Clarence J Palmer, 487th FS, Bodney, September 1943

3
P-47D-5 42-8491/*Donna Dae III* of Lt Leo Northrup, 486th FS, Bodney, November 1943

4
P-47D-5 42-8447/*"QUEEN CITY MAMA"* of Capt Donald K Dilling, 487th FS, Bodney, December 1943

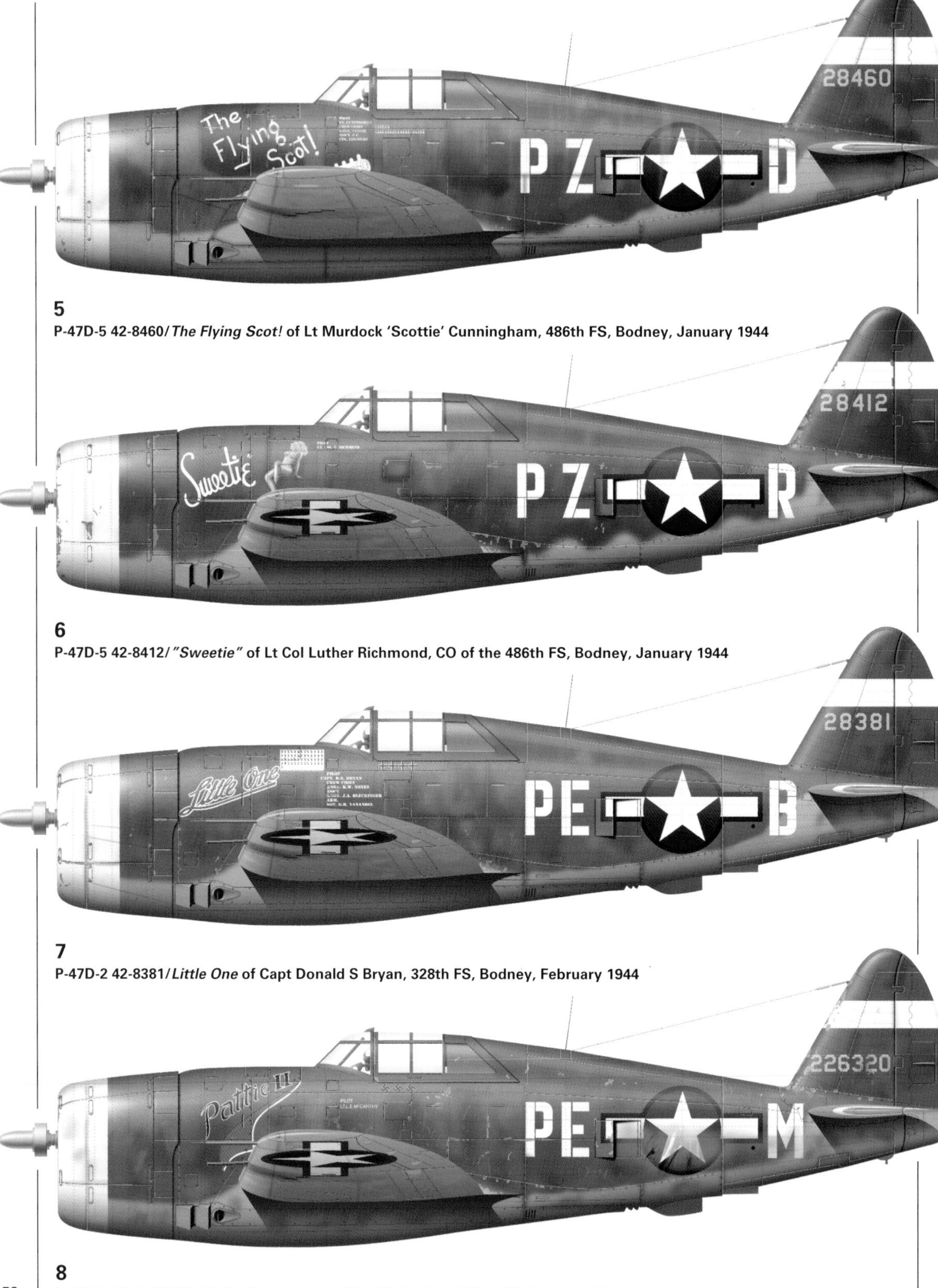

5

P-47D-5 42-8460/*The Flying Scot!* of Lt Murdock 'Scottie' Cunningham, 486th FS, Bodney, January 1944

6

P-47D-5 42-8412/*"Sweetie"* of Lt Col Luther Richmond, CO of the 486th FS, Bodney, January 1944

7

P-47D-2 42-8381/*Little One* of Capt Donald S Bryan, 328th FS, Bodney, February 1944

8

P-47D-5 42-26320/*Pattie II* of Lt Lawrence 'Mac' McCarthy, 328th FS, Bodney, February 1944

9
P-47D-5 42-8439/*Slender, Tender and Tall* of Capt William T Halton, 328th FS, Bodney, February 1944

10
P-47D-5 42-8473/*Sweet LOUISE/Mrs Josephine/Hedy* of Capt Virgil K Meroney, 487th FS, Bodney, March 1944

11
P-51B-15 42-106832/*WE THREE* of Lt Edmond Zellner, 328th FS, Bodney, May 1944

12
P-51B-5 43-6685/*Umbriago* of Lt Robert Frascotti, 486th FS, Bodney, May 1944

13

P-51B-5 43-6704/*HELL-ER-BUST* of Lt Edwin Heller, 486th FS, Bodney, May 1944

14

P-51B-10 42-106661/*Hot Stuff* of Maj Willie O Jackson Jr, CO of the 486th FS, Bodney, May 1944

15

P-51B-5 43-7022/*Little Rebel* of Lt Alton J 'Al' Wallace, 486th FS, Bodney, May 1944

16

P-51B-10 42-106483/*Miss Lace* of Lt Donald McKibben, 486th FS, Bodney, May 1944

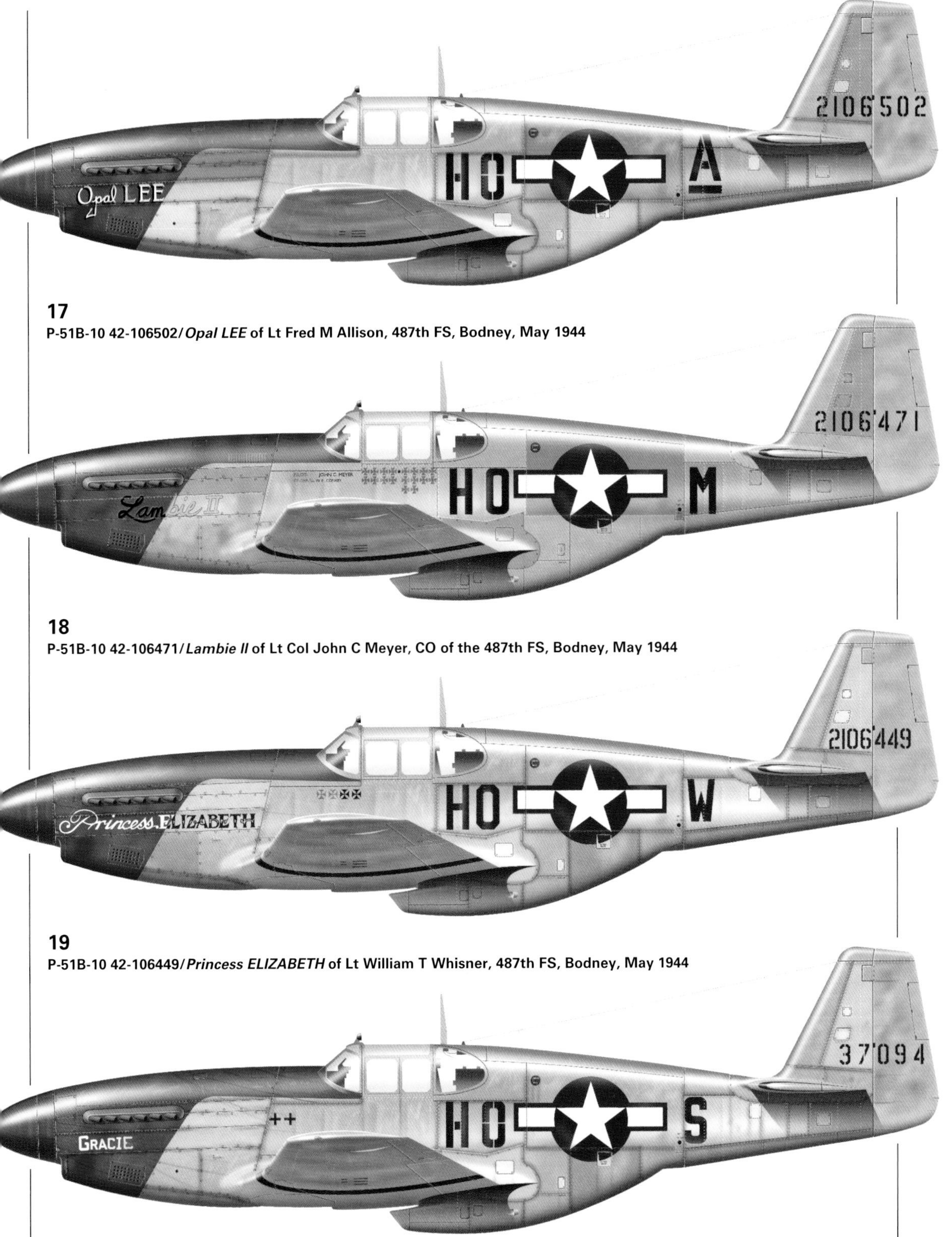

17
P-51B-10 42-106502/*Opal LEE* of Lt Fred M Allison, 487th FS, Bodney, May 1944

18
P-51B-10 42-106471/*Lambie II* of Lt Col John C Meyer, CO of the 487th FS, Bodney, May 1944

19
P-51B-10 42-106449/*Princess ELIZABETH* of Lt William T Whisner, 487th FS, Bodney, May 1944

20
P-51B-5 43-7094/G*RACIE*/*Josephine* of Lt Malcolm Pickering, 487th FS, Bodney, May 1944

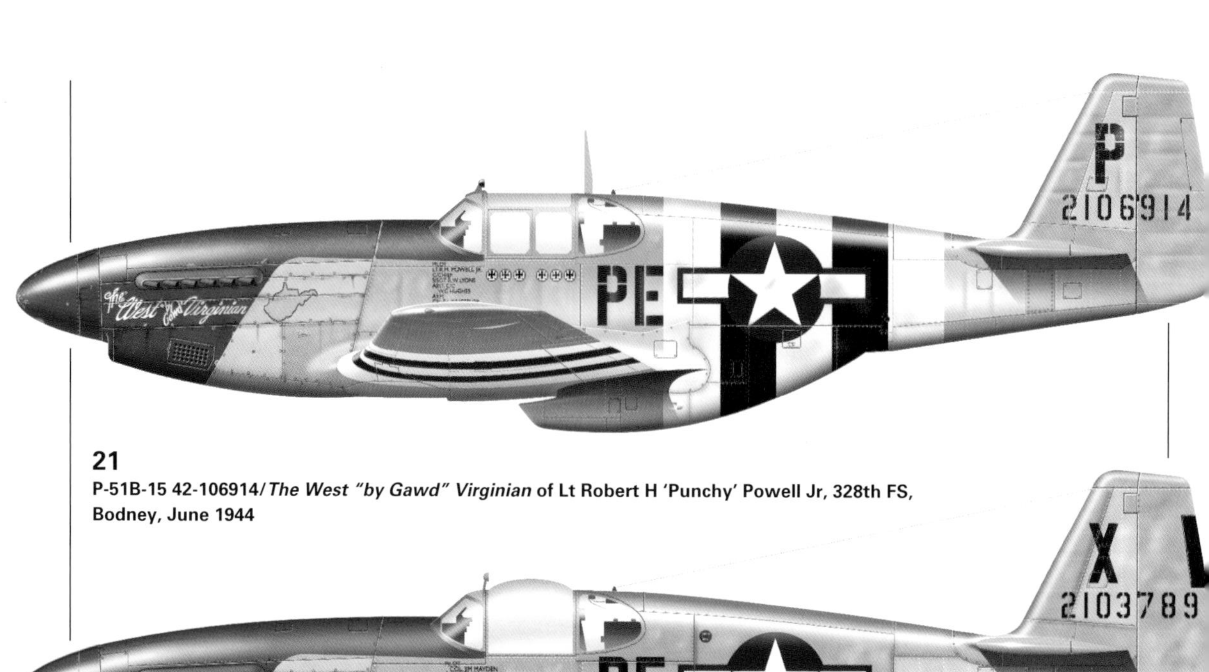

21
P-51B-15 42-106914/*The West "by Gawd" Virginian* of Lt Robert H 'Punchy' Powell Jr, 328th FS, Bodney, June 1944

22
P-51C-10 42-103789/*Straw Boss* of Lt Col James D Mayden, HQ 352nd FG, Bodney, Summer 1944

23
P-51B-10 42-106472/*The FLYING SCOT*!!/*Vicious Virgie* of Lt Carlton Fuhrman, 486th FS, Bodney, June 1944

24
P-51C-5 42-103758/*The FOX* of Lt James N Wood, 487th FS, Bodney, June 1944

25
P-51B-15 43-24807/*STARCK MAD!/Even Stevens* of Capt Walter 'Wally' Starck, 487th FS, Bodney, June 1944

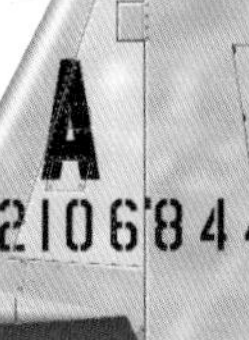

26
P-51B-15 42-106844/*Flossie II* of Maj Earl Abbott, 328th FS, Bodney, July 1944

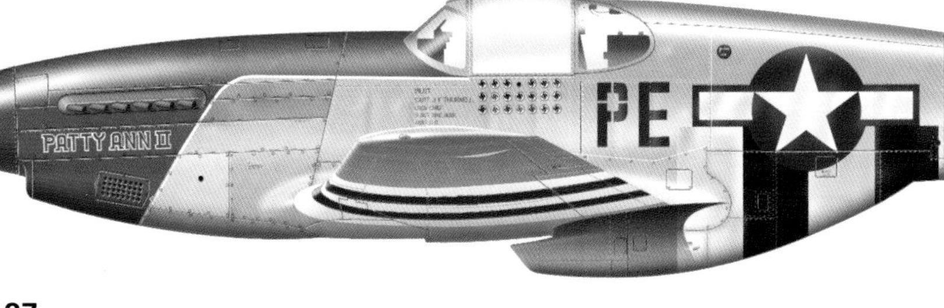

27
P-51B-15 42-106872/*PATTY ANN II* of Lt John F Thornell, 328th FS, Bodney, July 1944

28
P-51D-10 44-14151/*PETIE 2ND* of Lt Col John C Meyer, CO of the 487th FS, Bodney, August 1944

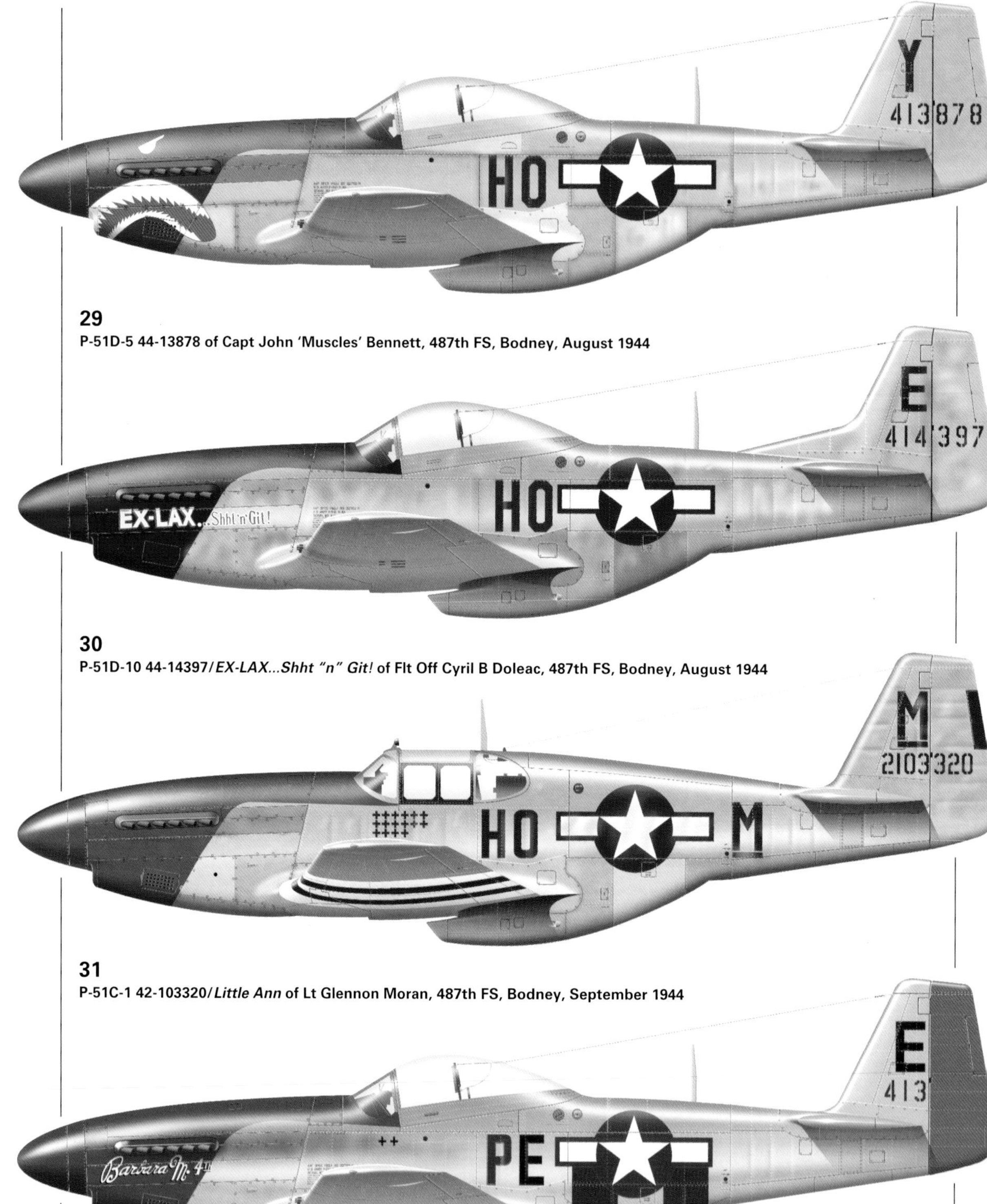

29
P-51D-5 44-13878 of Capt John 'Muscles' Bennett, 487th FS, Bodney, August 1944

30
P-51D-10 44-14397/*EX-LAX...Shht "n" Git!* of Flt Off Cyril B Doleac, 487th FS, Bodney, August 1944

31
P-51C-1 42-103320/*Little Ann* of Lt Glennon Moran, 487th FS, Bodney, September 1944

32
P-51D-5 44-13406/*Barbara M. 4TH* of Lt Col John 'Curly' Edwards, CO of the 328th FS, Bodney, September 1944

33
P-51D-10 44-14061/*Little One III* of Capt Donald S Bryan, 328th FS, Bodney, November 1944

34
P-51D-15 44-14877/*PENNIE'S EARL* of Lt Earl Lazear, 486th FS, Bodney, November 1944

35
P-51D-5 44-11330/*E Pluribus Unum* of Lt Raymond Littge, 487th FS, Bodney, November 1944

36
P-51D-5 44-13401/*Diann Ruth II* of Capt Charles Cesky, 328th FS, Asch (Y-29), Belgium, December 1944

37

P-51D-15 44-14906/*Cripes A'Mighty* of Maj George E Preddy, CO of the 328th FS, Asch (Y-29), Belgium, December 1944

38

P-51D-15 44-15041/*PETIE 3RD* of Lt Col John C Meyer, Deputy CO of the 352nd FG, Asch (Y-29), Belgium, December 1944

39

P-51D-10 44-14815/*Stinky 2* of Capt William J Stangel, 328th FS, Asch (Y-29), Belgium, January 1945

40

P-51D-10 44-14237/*Moonbeam McSWINE* of Capt William T Whisner, 487th FS, Asch (Y-29), Belgium, January 1945

41
P-51D-15 44-15041/*Ricky* of Lt James N Wood, 487th FS, Asch (Y-29), Belgium, January 1945

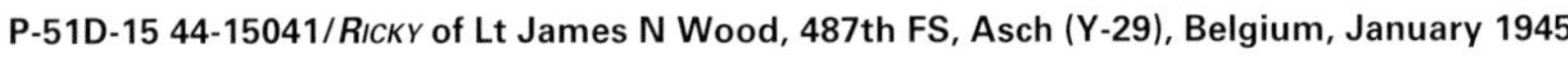

42
P-51D-5 44-13530/*Dutchess* of Capt Duerr Schuh, 487th FS, Chiévres (Y-84), Belgium, March 1945

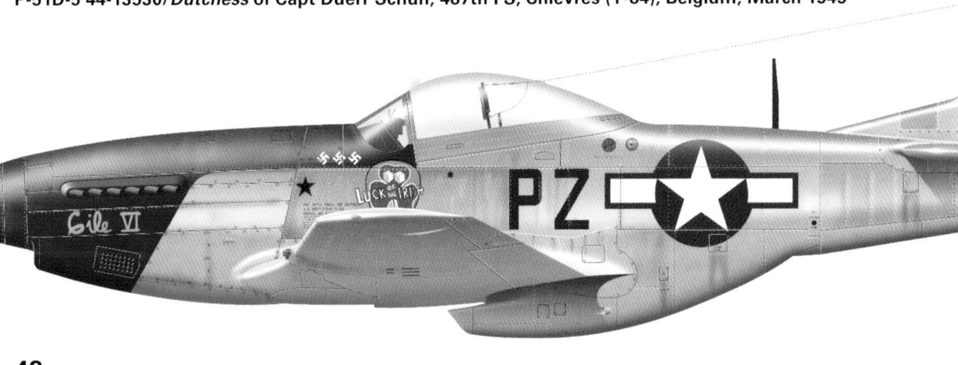

43
P-51D-15 44-15611/*Cile VI*/*LUCK of the IRISH* of Capt Chester V Harker, 486th FS, Chiévres (Y-84), Belgium, April 1945

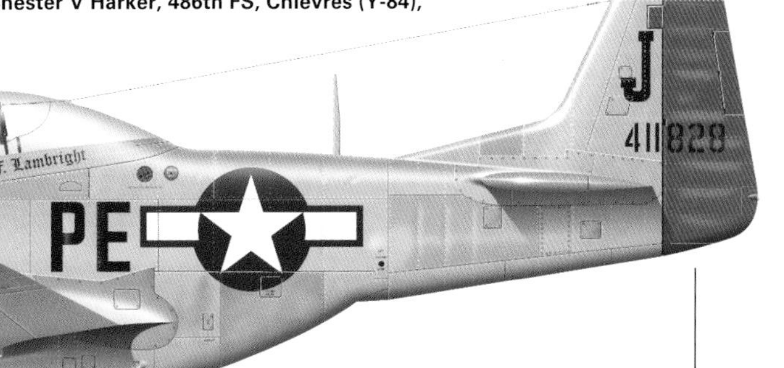

44
P-51K-5 44-11828/*Geraldine II* of Lt James F 'Duke' Lambright, 328th FS, Bodney, April 1945

45

P-51D-5 44-13806/*KENTUCKY BABE* of Lt Steve Price, 328th FS, Bodney, April 1945

46

P-51K 44-11626/*"It's SUPERMOUSE"*/Sweet Sue of Lt Robert W 'Bobby' Dodd, 328th FS, Bodney, April 1945

47

P-51D-10 44-14696/*HELL-ER-BUST* of Capt Edwin L Heller, 486th FS, Bodney, April 1945

48

P-51D-5 44-13737/Little Rebel of Lt Charles C 'Buck' Pattillo, 486th FS, Bodney, April 1945

49

P-51D-10 44-14812/*Slender Tender & TALL* of Maj William T Halton, CO of the 487th FS, Bodney, April 1945

50

P-51K-5 44-11556/*Sweet AND Lovely* of Lt Cuthbert A 'Bill' Pattillo, 487th FS, Bodney, April 1945

51

Noorduyn C-64A Norseman 44-70380/*JOY RIDE*, 328th FS, Bodney, Spring 1945

1
21st Fighter Squadron

2
328th Fighter Squadron

3
486th Fighter Squadron

4
487th Fighter Squadron

D-DAY TO *MARKET-GARDEN*

With Allied aerial superiority now clearly established, the path to the long awaited invasion of Europe was at last clear. During the first few days of June 1944 the 352nd FG flew five missions to targets in Occupied Europe. All were uneventful, except for the mission of 5 June, when Lt William Furr of the 328th FS was shot down by flak near St Omer, in France, and was captured.

A second mission on this day was scrubbed, and the base was put on full alert. This coincided with the rapid application of mysterious black and white stripes around the wings and fuselages of the group's Mustangs, leaving the residents of Bodney airfield in little doubt that the invasion was imminent.

D-Day began at 0230 hrs for the 352nd FG, and the opening moments of the day were marred by an accident so horrific that it remains seared in the memories of anyone who witnessed it.

Temporary lights had been laid out to illuminate the runway during the dark and misty early pre-dawn hours. Unfortunately, as the initial flight of four 486th FS Mustangs took off, one of its aircraft hit the lights and knocked them out. The next flight, now shrouded in darkness, lined up off centre, and as they accelerated down the runway Lt Robert Frascotti's fully fuelled P-51B crashed into the new, and as yet unfinished, control tower and exploded into flames. Positioned alongside Frascotti was his flightmate Lt Carlton Fuhrman, whose fighter had literally just taken off;

The ill-fated Lt Robert Frascotti of the 486th FS stands alongside his P-51B-5 43-6685 *Umbriago* in April 1944. He was killed in a take-off accident in this machine in the early hours of D-Day morning (*Marc Hamel*)

P-51B-10 42-106451 'HO-R' was assigned to Lt Carl Tafel of the 487th FS at the time of the D-Day landings. It had formerly been Maj George Preddy's *Cripes A'Mighty*, and although the fighter was recoded, Tafel had not got around to having his predecessor's scoreboard touched out! The name *Cripes A'Mighty* was also still carried on the nose, but it is not visible in this photo. Lt Jule Conard was forced to bail out of this machine when it suffered a mechanical failure over Munich on 16 July (*Carla Dimmitt via Sam Sox*)

'At first I was going to let my Mustang stay down a little longer, but a voice in my mind was shouting at me to "keep it up, keep it up" as I flew along watching the wing lights of Frascotti's plane to my left, and slightly below me. Suddenly an enormous fireball appeared. I saw two streams of fire spread out, and I thought that someone had dropped their wing tanks and they had exploded. There was no time to do anything but fly through the flames. Thank Heaven that good old Merlin engine never missed a beat. When I came out of the flames I was momentarily blinded by the darkness, and I pulled back on the stick to gain altitude. The plane's shudder warned me of an impending stall, and I hoped that I would be able to see my instruments before I lost control. It seemed a long time, but was probably only a few seconds before I could see my instruments and get control again.'

A number of tributes were later written about Lt Frascotti by his squadronmates, with Lt Charles Griffith entitling his 'The Guiding Light' in reference to his friend's crash, and the ensuing fire that brightened the night sky, enabling the remaining fighters to take off without incident. Just 21 years of age, Bob Frascotti was due to return home following the completion of this mission (his 89th in the ETO).

On D-Day the 352nd's pilots flew 116 sorties over the invasion front, and inflicted considerable damage to the German war machine. Included in the day's tally was the destruction of two enemy aircraft and numerous motor vehicles. The aerial victories were claimed south-east of Rouen by the 328th FS's Lt Richard Brookins, who downed an Fw 190, and Lts Leroy Allain and Francis Horne, who shared credit for a Focke-Wulf fighter – this was the latter pilot's final aerial claim of the war, raising his tally to 5.5 kills. Tempering this success was the loss of two 487th pilots to flak during the last mission of the day. Lt Robert O'Nan became a PoW and Lt Robert Butler returned to the 352nd.

The next day's missions were to prove even more costly to the group, with no fewer than four aircraft being lost and four pilots being killed – the highest single day loss of life in combat for the 352nd FG in the entire war. Hardest hit once again was the 487th, which suffered three of the fatalities. The first, Lt William Mulkey, was lost shortly after take-off when his bomb-laden Mustang crashed and exploded. Lt Robert Hall fell next, his Mustang hit by flak near Argentan. Finally, Lt Clifford Garney spun in over England on the return flight to Bodney.

The fourth pilot lost of 7 June was Maj Edward Gignac, who was one of the 486th FS's oldest and most experienced pilots. A veteran of the Pacific theatre, he was on his second sortie of the day when his P-51B was set on fire by flak whilst strafing a truck convoy near Le Merlerault. The fighter crashed before Gignac could bail out.

This impressive line-up photograph was taken at Debden on 16 June 1944. The P-51B/Cs of the 486th FS Mustangs had flown down to the home of the 4th FG in preparation for the first 'Shuttle Mission' to the USSR, but bad weather had caused the operation to be postponed. The sole D-model Mustang in this view is P-51D-5 44-13398, which had only been delivered to Bodney several days earlier. It was assigned to 486th FS CO Maj Willie O Jackson (who used it to claim three kills on 18-19 July), and by the time the 'Shuttle Mission' began on 21 June, the 352nd's distinctive swept back blue nose marking had been added to 44-13398 (*Air Force Museum*)

The strafing and bombing missions over the invasion front lasted for another ten days, and continued to inflict unprecedented losses on the group. The 328th had Lts John Campbell and Harry Miller killed in action on the 8th, while the 486th lost Lt Ted Fahrenwald to flak, although he successfully evaded. The following day bad weather claimed the lives of Lts Robert Sharp and Lt Richard Pratt from the 328th FS when their Mustangs almost certainly collided in heavy cloud. Finally, on 10 June Lt Raymond Phillips from the 328th FS was shot down and killed by flak, while Lt Donald Markle (from the 486th) died when his P-51 hit trees while strafing.

Lt Lincoln Bundy from the 486th FS was also downed by flak on the 10th, and although he was rescued by French partisans, his freedom was cut short when he and his French benefactors were captured and executed by the Germans on 7 July.

Despite these losses, the 352nd continued to pound ground targets, and on 12 June its pilots claimed three aerial victories over France.

During this period planning for the first of the long range 'Shuttle Missions' to the USSR was under preparation, and the 486th FS was selected to accompany the 4th FG on this historic flight. The first mission was originally scheduled for 16 June, but was postponed due to poor weather. The 486th returned to Bodney and awaited orders for the next attempt.

In the meantime the unit participated in an escort mission to Magdeburg on 20 June. Upon arrival in the target area, the 352nd found a mixed force consisting of 12 Ju 88s and about 24 Bf 109s waiting for them. The 486th charged into the German formation, and Maj Stephen Andrew's White Flight destroyed four aircraft. Lt Lester Howell reported the action;

'I was flying White 4 in a four-ship flight when I called out 20+ aeroplanes at three o'clock to us. We turned 180 degrees and came in behind them. They were Me-109s heading into the bombers on the left side. They broke for the deck upon sighting us, with the exception of one machine which broke left. Maj Andrew's wingman and White 3 started after the diving fighters. The '109 that broke left tried to get on my tail as I started down covering White 3 (Lt Brashear). I broke sharply so he split-essed and headed for the deck. I kept turning above Brashear, giving him cover.

'At this time Lt (Waldo) Raub – White 2 – collided with an Me-109 and both aeroplanes exploded. No 'chutes were seen. Lt Brashear gave me cover and I turned inside a '109. I took a short deflection burst at 200 yards but missed. I then moved in closer and got in a good burst from dead astern, observing hits on the wing roots. At 100 ft the pilot bailed out and his 'chute did not open. His aeroplane crashed in a field. I strafed the crashed aeroplane before rejoining the flight and gaining altitude.

'We then sighted 20+ aeroplanes on an airfield near Burg. There were Ju 52s, Ju 88s and, in the main, He 177s. We strafed the field and Maj Andrew, who was flight leader, set a Ju 52 on fire – it was burning when I passed over the field. I had one gun firing and got strikes on a He 177.'

Lt Brashear also destroyed a Ju 88 during the strafing run.

The 487th FS had also found a number of targets in the air on this day, with Maj George Preddy getting things going by downing an Fw 190 in a short fight, and then sharing in the destruction of an Me 410 with his wingman, Lt James N Wood. Before the 487th broke off combat Capt Walter Starck shot up an Fw 190 and claimed it as a probable and Lt Robert Berkshire damaged an Me 410. Upon returning from this mission the 486th FS learned that the 'Shuttle Mission' was on again, and the 18 selected pilots headed for Debden.

The weather did not look good on the morning of 21 June 1944. A heavy overcast blanketed the airfield, and many of the pilots expected the mission to again be scrubbed. Their doubts were short-lived though as a new weather forecast assured them that good weather would accompany them all the way to Russia. At 0755 hrs Col Don Blakeslee led his reinforced 4th FG away from Debden and toward its rendezvous point with the bombers over Leszno, in Poland.

The link-up with the 'heavies' was made right on schedule, and the formations continued towards their targets unmolested for about an hour. Then at about 1240 hrs a gaggle of enemy aircraft attacked the bombers. The mixed force of red- and blue-nosed Mustangs spotted the fighters and quickly intervened, destroying six – the 486th claimed four of these victories. The action was described by Lt Donald McKibben;

'Warsaw had passed under our wings 20 minutes before when the '109s came. There were 15+ of them, and most of them never got to attack. The few that did never returned because P-51s were hot on their tails. Lt Northrup accounted for two, Lts Whinnem and Heller one apiece, and Maj Andrew damaged another. We were pleased with our showing, as the three squadrons of the 4th FG tallied only one or two Huns for the loss of one P-51. The '109s gave us a break by delaying their attack until we had run our external tanks dry, so we didn't waste any gas.'

After this engagement ended Col Blakeslee led his group on to its temporary airbase at Piryatin, in Russia.

P-51C-5 42-103758 *The FOX* ('HO-Z') was Lt James N Wood's first assigned Mustang. This aircraft seemed to lead a 'charmed life', for Wood flew at least 45 missions in it during the summer and early autumn of 1944, before receiving his first 'bubble-top' Mustang (P-51D-15 44-15041). 42-103758 continued to serve with the 487th FS until war's end, being flown by numerous pilots during its lengthy spell in the frontline (*William Kohlhas*)

Mechanics from the 486th FS look over 'Bud' Fuhrman's well-weathered P-51B *The FLYING SCOT II* after it had landed in Russia at the end of the first leg of the 'Shuttle Mission' (*Carleton Fuhrman*)

The second leg of the 'Shuttle Mission' completed, Col Blakeslee's task force settled down in Italy. This view shows a mixed group of 4th FG and 486th FS Mustangs at the 52nd FG's Madna base on the Adriatic coast (*Carleton Fuhrman*)

After a few days in the USSR, where the Americans had endured a bombing raid by the Germans and enjoyed lavish meals and ceremonies from the Russians, Blakeslee's fighters headed out on the second leg of the 'Shuttle Mission'. This 1100-mile leg would take them over Poland, where the bombers would hit oil refineries, before heading to Italy.

This part of the mission turned out to be a 'milk run' for the 486th, and after landing in Italy things got even better, for the pilots were able to relax on the beaches of the Adriatic Sea for a few days. The 'vacation' came to an abrupt end on 2 July when Blakeslee's group headed for Budapest, in Hungary. Their mission was to sweep the target area before the Fifteenth Air Force bombers arrived, and then provide target area support.

Just as the 'heavies' began their bomb run a large gaggle of enemy aircraft was observed and the fight was on. Capt Don Higgins led the 486th into the fray, shooting down an Fw 190 in a brief encounter. Higgins then followed up this kill with a shared victory over a Bf 109.

Unfortunately, Capt Higgins' victories were overshadowed by the loss of two 486th pilots during the engagement. Lt Lester Howell was shot down and killed during a dogfight with Bf 109s, and eight-kill ace Maj Stephen Andrew became a PoW after his engine failed and he was forced to belly land deep inside enemy territory. The 4th FG lost five pilots during the engagement, two of whom were killed. One of the those to die was the irrepressible 15-kill ace Lt Ralph 'Kidd' Hofer.

The last two missions of the 'Shuttle' proved to be uneventful, and ended when the Blakeslee force arrived back at Debden on 5 July. For its part, the 486th had destroyed 5.5 aircraft during the 'Shuttle' mission for the loss of two of its own. Most importantly, the unit had helped prove that 'Shuttle' missions could indeed be flown, thus paving the way for the future long range strategic bombing campaign that followed.

The remaining units of the 352nd FG had not been idle during this period (21-29 June), flying eight missions and claiming nine aerial and four strafing victories, as well as destroying numerous targets on the ground.

On 21 June the 328th and 487th engaged a mixed force of Me 410s and Bf 109s near Magdeburg, the former taking on the twin-engined fighters

Mustangs of the 328th FS await their next mission over the Invasion Front in June. P-51B-10 42-106703 'PE-S' was Lt Francis Horne's *Snoot's Sniper*. This machine's nickname (on the port side only) was misspelled, as it was supposed to be *Snoot's Snipper* – the fighter's crew chief was S/Sgt Art Snyder, who doubled as the 328th FS's barber! Note the barber's pole forward of the wing. Another long-lived machine, 42-106703 accumulated over 300 flying hours, and was still at Bodney come VE-Day (*352nd FG Association*)

Above
These finless M-43 500-lb General Purpose bombs will soon be towed out to the flightline and secured to the D-Day striped Mustangs visible in the background. Note the positioning of the single letter code on these aircraft, the 487th preferring to stencil the letter onto the fin whilst the 486th have painted it on just aft of the exhaust stubs (*via Michael O'Leary*)

Right
Bare metal Mustangs of the 487th FS prepare to shoulder the weight of yet more 500 'pounders' at Bodney in July 1944. Note how the stripes have been left on the undersides of the wings of both fighters, but removed from the fuselage. The Mustang in the middle of this photograph is P-51B-15 42-106836, assigned to Capt John Kessler (who would finish his ETO tour the following month – he had joined the squadron in the US in 1943) (*via Michael O'Leary*)

and destroying two of them. Both were shared victories, one being destroyed by Lts John Thornell and Sammy Dyke and the other by Lts Elmer Smith and John Galiga. The Bf 109s did not escape the watchful eyes of the 487th either, and two were shot down by Maj George Preddy and Lt Glennon Moran.

The 487th FS managed four more aerial victories on 27 June during a mission over France. The dogfight took place north of Noyan when Red Flight, led by Lt Robert Berkshire, bounced four Fw 190s at 3000 ft and

This heavily posed shot shows Capt Walter 'Wally' Starck inspecting belted 0.50-in ammunition with his groundcrew (from left to right), crew chief Keith Stevens, Robert McKinney and William McCurtain. They are standing in front of their P-51B-15 43-24807 *Starck Mad!*, which Starck used to claim two of his seven kills. This photograph was taken in July 1944, the very month that Starck scored his victories (both Bf 109s) with this aircraft. Note the differing tread pattern on the main wheel tyres (*Walter Starck*)

Another shot of 'Wally' Starck's P-51B-15 43-24807 *Starck Mad!*, taken some weeks prior to the photograph above The fighter is devoid of the 352nd's distinctive blue nose marking, as well as its nose-art and three of the four crosses applied beneath the cockpit. The solitary victory symbol seen here denotes the pilot's single P-47 kill, scored on 10 February 1944 (*via Michael O'Leary*)

destroyed them all. Two victories were credited to Lt Jule Conard and Lts Charles Corson and Alex Sears claimed one apiece. Lt Berkshire (4.5 aerial kills and 5.5 strafing victories) disappeared during the combat and was later reported as a PoW. Two other pilots from the 487th were lost during the last days of June, Flt Off William Drisko evading capture after being shot down by a Bf 109 over Soissons on the 25th, and Lt Adolf Bielok losing his life when shot down by flak whilst strafing targets near St Omer on the 28th.

During the first five days of July VIII Fighter Command directed its aircraft to attack *No Ball* targets (launch sites for rocket-powered V1 pilotless flying bombs) in France. On 1 July Capt Wally Starck led 28 P-51s to France to strafe a number of these sites in the Pas de Calais area, but upon arriving at the target area he was diverted to an air battle 30 miles away.

When Starck's force arrived in the St Quentin area, they found an air battle already taking place between the 78th FG and a gaggle of about 20 Bf 109s. Without hesitation, Starck attacked a pair of Messerschmitts which had tried, unsuccessfully, to turn inside him before heading for the deck. The Mustang pilot followed, opening fire at a distance of 100 yards. The Bf 109 burst into flames and its pilot bailed out, narrowly missing Lt Sheldon Heyer's P-51. Starck then turned his attention to the other Messerschmitt, and he succeeded in damaging it before he lost the fighter in the clouds. Two other Bf 109s were also damaged, these claims being filed by Lt Cyrus Greer of the 487th and Lt Robert Powell of the 328th.

This air battle turned out to be the last that the 'Bluenosers' would see for over a week, with no enemy aircraft being encountered during the eight missions flown between 4-12 July. Indeed, about the only news of note to report during this period was the arrival of Lt Col James D Mayden, the 352nd's new Group Executive Officer.

The group returned to escort duty on 13 July and destroyed one of the Bf 109s it encountered near Schweigenhausen, in Germany. Lt Col John Edwards' encounter report stated;

Lt Col James D Mayden became Group Executive Officer in early July 1944, and then assumed overall command on the 24th of that month when Col Joe Mason returned to the US on 30 days' leave. He is seen here with crew chief, S/Sgt Hubert Robling (*Sheldon Berlow*)

Lt Col John 'Curly' Edwards' *Barbara M 4th* first flew as 'HO-E' while its pilot was assigned to the 487th FS. When he assumed command of the 328th FS on 22 July 1944, Edwards brought the fighter (P-51D-5 44-13406) with him, and it became 'PE-E'. The P-51 was later assigned to Lt Alvin Chesser who renamed it *BAMA REBEL*. A fin strake was also added at this time (*352nd FG Association*)

'The enemy acted aggressively and pulled up after their pass (at the B-17s). I observed one '109, which I thought to be their airborne controller, climbing above the other '109s, and I turned after him. I flew underneath him and closed very rapidly from astern. I opened fire and my bullets struck the cockpit, causing the enemy aircraft to explode and tumble back toward me. I dived under it to avoid it and saw the enemy aircraft burning, debris falling from it, and going into an uncontrollable spin. All the other enemy aircraft dived for the protective cloud cover.'

This encounter ended contact with the Luftwaffe until 18 July, and although three uneventful missions had been flown between the 14th and 17th, they were not without loss. Lt Jule Conard's engine failed over Munich during the mission of 16 July and he was forced to bail out near Aalen. He was quickly captured.

The brief period of 'milk runs' came to an end on the 18th when the 352nd escorted bombers to targets in Peenemünde and Zinnowitz. Approaching Warnemünde, the 'Bluenosers', led by Maj Willie O Jackson, encountered a large force of enemy aircraft that had been stalking the bombers for some time.

The German formation was a mixed force of about 40 Me 410s and Ju 88s, with a top cover of 20 Bf 109s. Despite being outnumbered, the 486th and 487th FSs charged into the gaggle of twin-engined interceptors and quickly dispersed them, while the 328th engaged the Bf 109s. No fewer than 19 enemy fighters were claimed shot down and another 11 damaged.

As was often the case, Maj George Preddy led the scoring with two Ju 88s destroyed and a third as a probable (and two more Junkers 'twins' damaged), plus a solitary Bf 109 shot down. These successes raised his tally of aerial victories to 14.5. For Lt Charles Ellison of the 487th FS, this was the most exciting day of his tour of duty. After flying over 70 missions without a kill, he downed three Ju 88s in quick succession. Other successful 487th FS pilots were Lt William Fowler, who claimed two Bf 109s destroyed, and Lt Sanford Moats who got a single Messerschmitt fighter.

The 486th also boosted its score with a further seven victories. Four of these kills were credited to young pilots who had only joined the squadron in May or June. Lts Ernest Bostrom, Robert Miller and David French each destroyed an Me 410, while Lts Marvin Stoll and David Reichman claimed a Ju 88 apiece. Proving, however, that combat experience still counted for something, squadron CO Maj Willie O Jackson was the only pilot from the 486th to claim both a Ju 88 and a Bf 109 destroyed.

The Luftwaffe's bomber destroyers had fared badly at the hands of the 352nd on this day, and its single-engined fighters suffered much the same fate, with seven being lost. Three of the Bf 109s downed fell to Capt Henry White and Lts Frank Kebelman and Earl Smith of the 328th FS.

This unit also suffered the only combat losses of the 18th when Lts John Galiga and James Burr were both shot down and killed – the latter pilot was flying P-51D-5 44-13320 at the time of his death, this fighter being the first D-model to be lost by the group in combat.

The 352nd had come very close to losing a third pilot at the very outset of the mission when Lt Robert 'Punchy' Powell crash-landed his fully fuelled and armed P-51B near Bodney after its engine failed soon after take-off. Powell remembers;

Lt Robert H 'Punchy' Powell Jr of the 328th FS poses with his second fighter in the ETO, P-51B-15 42-106914 *The West "by Gawd" Virginian*. This aircraft was totally destroyed when its engine failed on take-off on 18 July 1944, Powell at that point being just six missions short of finishing his second combat tour (*Robert H Powell Jr*)

'With no power and no more airfield, I was descending rapidly into a line of tall trees in front of me. Although trained to land straight ahead when losing power on take-off, I skidded the plane in a turn of about 45 degrees to make it into an open field to avoid those trees. In a complete "panic" mode in those seconds, I kicked it back out of the turn as I felt the stall coming and bellied it in as flames mushroomed all around me.

'I had been too busy stretching my glide in that turn to open my canopy, but it turned out to be a good belly landing. There wasn't too much time to pat myself on the back though, as the flames which had been temporarily knocked down by the nose ploughing through the soft field flared up again. I tried to open the canopy but it wouldn't budge. I pulled the emergency release and tried to push it off – no luck. The "panic factor" quadrupled. I jerked everything loose – radio cord, oxygen mask connection, seat and shoulder straps – doubled my legs up as I slid down into the bucket seat and gave the canopy a super kick with both feet. The canopy fell off to one side and I jumped up and off the wing and ran like crazy. Fortunately my flight clothes did not catch fire as I ran from the explosion that I expected to happen.

'I ran through the woods to a small road that led back to the 328th area and followed it to the pilots' hut. Dave Lee, our S-2 (Intelligence Officer), was on the crank phone talking to headquarters, and I heard him say, "It was 'Punchy'. and it looks like he's had it". Then seeing me, he said with a startled expression, "No he's okay, he just walked in here."

'Dave and I got into his jeep and rode down to the crash site after he saw I was okay. As we stopped near Doc Lemon, the flight surgeon, I yelled, "Hey Doc! Who was it?" Before looking up he said "Punchy", then realised that he was talking to me. Surprised, he said "How the hell did you

The burned out cockpit section of P-51B-15 42-106914 *The West "by Gawd" Virginian* graphically illustrates just how lucky Lt Powell was to escape this fiery crash-landing. The panel which bore the aircraft's name survived the accident virtually untouched, and it is now mounted on the wall of 'Punchy's' 352nd FG Association 'War Room' (*Robert H Powell Jr*)

get out of that thing? We have been looking for your body all over the place!"

'He took me back to the hospital and checked me out and found that I was okay. After the exam, and a few prayers of thanks to my Maker, that was that.'

Lt Sanford 'Sandy' Moats and his P-51B-15 42-106751 'HO-U'. Although an ace with 8.5 kills, Moats failed to lodge a single claim with this particular aircraft. He is another of the 352nd FG's alumni that rose to the rank of general in the post-war USAF (*352nd FG Association*)

Action continued on 19 July when the 352nd engaged a flight of 20 Bf 109s near Munich and destroyed eight of them. Most of the damage was done by the 486th, whose pilots claimed seven kills and two damaged. Capt Lloyd Rauk and Lts Earl Mundell and Lumir Vitek each destroyed two Bf 109s, and the seventh kill fell to Maj Jackson, taking the CO's tally to four aerial victories. The eighth victory of the day was scored by Lt Robert Draftz of the 487th FS. One Mustang was lost on the trip back to Bodney when the engine of Lt William Wilson's fighter failed due to fuel starvation. Having only joined the 328th FS earlier in the month, Wilson's tour came to a premature end when he parachuted into captivity.

The 'Bluenosers' escorted bombers of the 3rd Air Division to Regensburg on 21 July, and again encountered some resistance from German fighters. At the rendezvous point, the 487th engaged a flight of ten Bf 109s and duly shot down three during a brief dogfight. Two of the bandits were destroyed in the initial attack by Capt Wally Starck (his fourth aerial kill) and Lt Malcolm Pickering, and the third was shared a few minutes later by Maj George Preddy and Lt Sandy Moats. Lt Pickering was brief and to the point in his encounter report;

'I was flying as White 3 when we attacked about ten Me-109s. I picked out one on the right of the formation. He was in a slight climb at about 28,000 ft, so I held my fire. He then started to dive and I opened fire at about 300 yards. I immediately noticed strikes in the engine and cockpit.

Lt David Zims and his groundcrew pose with their P-51B-10 42-106694 *Stinky*, coded 'PE-C', at Bodney in June 1944. Zims shot down a Bf 109 on 27 May 1944 while flying this aircraft. Assigned to the 328th in September 1943, Zims completed his ETO tour 11 months later (*352nd FG Association*)

He caught fire and trailed a huge cloud of white smoke. He then spun out of control and crashed. The pilot did not bail out.'

While this engagement was taking place, the other two squadrons continued their escort and observed excellent bombing results. From this point on, however, the remainder of the mission for the 328th FS proved to be disastrous. Shortly after breaking off from the bombers, the squadron ran into a thick overcast and strong headwinds, which hindered the homeward flight. Fuel consumption increased sharply as the 328th struggled against the hostile elements.

Upon reaching the North Sea, fuel gauges were already at the critical point and land was nowhere in sight. The pilots realised they were off course, and as they attempted to correct their heading, fuel tanks began running dry. The first to go down were three of the 328th's newer pilots (all had joined in June), Lts Richard Casper, Robert Lampman and James Lanter, all of whom vanished into the waters of the North Sea. Fate was much kinder, however, to Lts David Zims and Elmer Dubay when they bailed out a few minutes later north-east of Cromer, on the north Norfolk coast. Both men were promptly rescued by a US Navy minesweeper. Two more Mustangs force-landed along the English coastline, and neither pilot was seriously injured. Weather, not the Luftwaffe, had dealt the 328th FS its worst defeat of the war!

The next few days featured three uneventful missions and some major changes in command. Lt Col John Edwards replaced Maj Harold Lund as CO of the 328th FS and Lt Col James Mayden assumed command of the 352nd FG when Col Joe Mason headed home for a 30-day leave.

When the 352nd returned to Germany on 29 July, it encountered a large and aggressive force of enemy aircraft while escorting the Merseburg-bound 2nd Task Force (ten combat wings of B-17s). Within two minutes of rendezvousing with the bombers the 328th went into action. The first kill was credited to Lt Charles Bennette, leader of Blue Flight, who bounced a flight of Bf 109s just as they were making a pass at the bombers. He downed one of them without firing a shot, as noted in his encounter report;

When Lt Col John C Meyer returned from his leave in the United States as a newly-married man, his new P-51D-10 also received what is believed to be its 'married name'. This photo shows *PETIE 2ND* as it looked in August 1944, displaying 16 swastikas (8.5 of which were for aerial kills) and the aircraft's nickname in white, with a black outline. Meyer failed to score a single aerial victory with this machine, which was later passed on to Lt Sheldon Heyer, who renamed it *Sweetie FACE* (*via Michael O'Leary*)

'Just as I was ready to fire he pulled up sharply to the right. I continued my attack and the enemy aircraft did three or four high speed stalls. As he slowed down I noticed the canopy and other unidentified objects come out. He then went into a spin and I last observed him spinning down at about 16,000 ft. Lt Edmund Zellner saw the pilot of this enemy aircraft bail out.'

The second victory of the day went to future 8.5-kill ace Lt Charles Cesky of the 328th FS when he shot down an Fw 190 for his first success. Fifteen minutes later the 487th hunted down a gaggle of Bf 109s and claimed four more German fighters destroyed. Maj George Preddy, Capt Clarence Palmer and Lts Alexander Sears and Sandy Moats each destroyed a Messerschmitt, and with his kill Maj Preddy raised his score to 21.83. The 486th FS did not fare as well in this battle, losing Maj Gustav Lundquist (who was shot down by an Fw 190 and made a PoW) and having Lt David Reichman wounded, although he flew back to the UK.

With the victories of 29 July, the 352nd FG reached a new milestone in its history. The group had now destroyed 403.5 enemy aircraft, probably destroyed a further 20 and damaged 162. Maj George Preddy, with a total of 21.83 victories (15.83 aerial and six strafing), was now the 352nd's leading ace.

July 1944 was closed out with what was officially described as an 'uneventful mission', but if asked, Lts Edmond Zellner and MacDonald Godfrey of the 328th would have no doubt disagreed. Both men were shot down over Belgium by flak, with Godfrey becoming a PoW. Lt Zellner, who had volunteered to fly the mission (his 90th) in the place of a sick friend, successfully evaded capture and eventually made it back to Bodney after numerous adventures on the continent with the French Maquis.

Capt John Bennett's shark-mouthed P-51D-5 44-13878 was photographed whilst undergoing preparations for the boresighting of its guns at Bodney in the autumn of 1944 (*352nd FG Association*)

Even colonels have bad days! P-51C-10 42-103789 *StrawBoss*, flown by the 352nd's highly respected CO, Lt Col Jim Mayden, is photographed after its undignified wheels up landing at Bodney. Legend has it that warning flares and wave-offs went unnoticed by the colonel as he continued his 'gearless' approach. His gallant wingman, seeing what was happening, followed the boss's lead and brought his Mustang in the same way! The incident was written up as 'hydraulic failure', and some one in the group was later quoted as saying, 'Only the colonel knows why' (*352nd FG Association*)

Probably the most unusual, or at least unique, name for an aircraft in the 352nd FG was Flt Off Cyril Doleac's *EX-LAX...Shht"n"Git!*, alias P-51D-10 44-14397 'HO-E'. Inexplicably named after a well-known brand of laxative, a photograph of 44-14397 was displayed in the corporate headquarters of Ex-Lax during the war years (*Sheldon Berlow*)

August 1944 began with a series of uneventful *No Ball* missions to France, and more personnel changes at Bodney. The newly-married John C Meyer returned from his leave in the United States and reassumed command of the 487th FS. Along with him came three more 'old timers', Capts John Bennett and Clayton Davis and Lt Duncan Donohue.

Conversely, in the 328th and 486th many of the veteran pilots were headed home after completing their combat tours. The leadership arena in the 486th was hit especially hard as the list included the CO, Maj Willie Jackson, and four of his flight leaders – Capts Tom Colby and Martin Corcoran and Lts Ed Heller and Leo Northrup. The 328th lost Capt Henry White and Lts David Zims, Robert H Powell Jr, Lawrence McCarthy and Charles Bennette.

The 352nd resumed flying escort missions on 4 August, but was in the wrong place and missed out on the major battles that took place over Germany. The following day, however, the group was right in the thick of the action, and in a series of dogfights that lasted 20 minutes the 'Bluenosers' claimed five aircraft shot down, one probable and one damaged.

Maj Preddy started things off by shooting down a Bf 109 in flames and crippling a second Messerschmitt before he had to break off. As Preddy evaded the attack of a third Bf 109 on his tail, his squadron continued the assault, with Lt Alex Sears nailing the next fighter with four short bursts. Moments later Lts Glen Moran and Guy Taylor blasted two more Bf 109s out of the sky – this was Moran's 16th (13th in the air), and last, kill of the war. The German pilot had made every attempt to slip away from his pursuer, but could not break free. After several short bursts, Moran noted strikes on the wings and cockpit. The last sentence of his report stated, 'I believe the pilot was wounded by my fire because the aeroplane then went out of control and plunged straight into a field'.

The 486th FS also battled with the Bf 109s, Lt Don Whinnem claiming one as a probable and damaging another. Lt Don French followed this up by shooting down two Messerschmitts and damaging a third, before he was in turn shot down and captured. Lt Clifford Wilcox of the 487th also failed to return, and he was later reported KIA.

That evening, after learning the mission of 6 August would be scrubbed due to weather, a number of the pilots went to the Officers' Club to celebrate. George Preddy, in particular, had a great time, first winning $1200.00 in a crap game and then getting himself gloriously drunk! As often happens, weather can be fickle, and sure enough the skies cleared over Europe on the morning of the 6th and the mission was back on.

Maj Preddy had not been in bed an hour when the duty officer woke him for the mission. Aside from feeling decidely worse for wear, his problems multiplied when he remembered that it was his turn to lead the

352nd. Preddy was not a pretty sight at the briefing, but by take-off time he had managed to clear his head enough to fly the mission.

On the way to Germany Maj Preddy again began to feel the effects of the previous night, and he vomited in his cockpit. After this episode the ace began to feel a little better, and when he met the enemy 90 minutes later he was ready for action.

As the bomber stream approached Hamburg, a force of 30 Bf 109s began to stalk the 'heavies', and Maj Preddy led the bounce. Now fully alert, he led White Flight down to attack the Bf 109s from the rear. Preddy's encounter report tells the complete story of his historic day;

18 July 1944 was a big day for Maj George Preddy and P-51D-5 44-13321 *Cripes A'Mighty 3rd*. The four fingers indicated that he shot down three Ju 88s and a Bf 109 over Rostock, although one of the Junkers was later changed to a probable instead of confirmed. He would double this haul in the very same machine on 6 August. No fewer than 14 of Preddy's 26.833 aerial kills were claimed in this mustang between 20 June and 6 August (*Sheldon Berlow*)

'I opened fire on one near the rear of the formation from 300 yards and got many hits around the canopy. The enemy aircraft went down inverted and in flames. At this time, Lt Doleac became lost while shooting down an Me-109 that had latched onto Lt Heyer's tail. Lt Heyer and I continued our attack and I drove up behind another enemy aircraft, getting hits around the wing roots and setting him on fire after a short burst. He went spinning down and the pilot bailed out at 20,000 ft. I then saw Lt Heyer on my right shooting down another aircraft.

'The enemy formation stayed together taking practically no evasive action, and tried to get back for an attack on the bombers which were off to the right. We continued our attack on the rear end and I fired on another at close range. He went down smoking, and I saw him begin to fall apart below us. At this time four other P-51s came in to help us with the attack. I fired at another '109, causing him to burn after a short burst. He spiralled down to the right in flames. The formation headed down in a left turn, keeping themselves together in a rather close formation.

'I got a good burst into another one, causing him to burn and spin down. The enemy aircraft were down to 5000 ft now, and one pulled off to the left. I was all alone with them now, so I went after this single '109 before he could get on my tail. I got in an ineffective burst, causing him to smoke a little. I pulled up into a steep climb to the left above him and he climbed after me. I pulled it in as tight as possible and climbed at 150 mph. The Hun opened fire on me but could not get enough deflection to do any damage. With my initial speed, I slightly out-climbed him. He fell off to the left and I dropped astern of him. He jettisoned his canopy as I fired a short burst, getting many hits. As I pulled past,

Hit for six. The last of Maj Preddy's six kills looms large on the camera gun film automatically exposed when the ace pressed the fire button for his six 'fifties'. This shot was taken on 6 August 1944, and it helped prove that Maj Preddy had just set a new record for the 352nd FG by shooting down six Bf 109s in one mission (*352nd FG Association*)

the pilot bailed out at 7000 ft. I had lost contact with friendly and enemy aircraft, so I headed home. I claim SIX (6) Me-109s destroyed.'

The 328th and 486th FSs contributed four more kills, increasing the day's total to 12 destroyed. Two of the victories were claimed by the 486th's Capt Henry Miklajcyk, who was flying the first mission of his second tour – these claims took his tally of aerial kills to four. The remaining two victories were credited to Lt Charles Cesky of the 328th.

PETIE 2ND **is seen in its revised paint job, as per Lt Col Meyer's instructions. He had asked that the fighter's name and kill markings be repainted, with the previously white crosses and lettering reapplied in yellow, with a black outline. The lower portion of the lettering in the name was painted in orange, as can be seen in this photograph (*352nd FG Association*)**

When Maj Preddy landed after his record breaking mission, he was obviously still suffering from the night before. As soon as he rolled back his canopy an anxious crowd was there, asking him how many he had got. Preddy's reply was simply, 'NEVER AGAIN!' For these extraordinary feats of airmanship, Maj George Preddy was awarded the DSC, and immediately given a well earned leave to visit his family in the USA.

One pilot was lost on the mission and another on a routine training flight that same day. Lt Walter Gehrke of the 328th was killed when the wing of his Mustang came off as he dived to attack a Bf 109 east of Lüneburg, and Capt Quentin Quinn died when his Mustang inexplicably exploded in mid-air over Thetford, in Norfolk.

Quinn had been with the 328th FS since December 1942 and his death hit the squadron hard, as the unit historian noted;

'The loss of Quinn was keenly felt by all who knew him. The Squadron will certainly miss Quinn the pilot and Flight Leader, but more so the Squadron members will miss Quinn the man. A former candidate for the priesthood, Quinn travelled the road of life on its highest levels and evidenced many fine traits that were admired by his friends and associates. Often, a Quinn quip, led by its mock gravity, lightened the tenseness of a strained and troubled moment. With the Squadron from its beginning. Capt Quinn took great interest in any project or entertainment that affected the good of the Squadron. Ironically, the accident occurred only four days after his return from a 30-day leave period in the States.'

Following the memorable mission of 6 August, contact with the Luftwaffe evaporated for several days. During the period of 7-15 August the 'Bluenosers' hit ground targets in France, claiming a sizeable number of German vehicles, but at the cost of four more pilots. On the 12th Lt Robert Graham (487th) went down in France and became a PoW and Lt Gerald Thurman (486th) died after bailing out of his mechanically crippled Mustang over the Channel. Two more pilots were lost in strafing attacks the following day, Lt Leroy Allain (328th) being killed and Lt Harry Barnes (487th) becoming a PoW.

The 352nd FG returned to flying escort missions on 15 and 16 August, and claimed three aerial victories on the latter date. The first came after

Soon to be adorned with the nickname *The Sheep Herder* (note the titling chalked onto its blue nose below the exhaust stubs), P-51D-10 44-14778 'HO-E' was assigned to Lt Alex F Sears of the 487th FS. Transferred into the group in June 1944, Sears remained in the frontline with the 'Bluenosers' until June of the following year, by which time he had claimed five aerial kills (none in this machine) (*352nd FG Association*)

Capt Al Wallace of the 486th observed a flight of Bf 109s successfully attacking several B-17s. He chased two of the bandits as they broke for the ground and destroyed one of the them after catching it at 7000 ft.

Twenty minutes later the 487th engaged a gaggle of Fw 190s during a steep chase 'down to the deck'. Lt Pickering picked out the Focke-Wulf that had unsuccessfully attacked his wingman and hit the enemy fighter with a lethal burst at 10,000 ft. Large pieces broke away from the Fw 190 before it began its plunge to earth. The final kill of the day was shared between Capt Hendrian and Lts Cesky and Lambright. The German pilot was apparently totally oblivious of the Mustangs because all three of his assailants took it in turns to fall in behind the Bf 109 and systematically shoot it to pieces. Incredibly, the pilot of the Messerschmitt was not hit and bailed out successfully.

The return to ground support missions on 17 August cost the 352nd two more pilots – five-kill ace Capt Clayton Davis of the 487th and Lt Bill Reese of the 486th FS. Both men successfully evaded.

Between 18-24 August only two missions were flown, and the Luftwaffe was nowhere to be seen.

When the 352nd returned to Germany on the 25th, German fighters again refused to come up and fight, so the 'Bluenosers' went down after them. Lt Col Meyer led the 487th across an airfield near Neubrandenburg and his squadron destroyed seven aircraft and damaged five others. Meyer's claims were a Ju 52 and a He 177 destroyed. Strange as it may seem, these were the only victories J C Meyer would score in P-51D-10 44-14151, better known as *PETIE 2ND* – his most famous Mustang.

During the remainder of August the group encountered little opposition in the air, but still lost two pilots. Lt Charles Ferris of the 486th suffered a mechanical failure in his P-51 and bailed out over the Channel but was never found, and Lt Carl Fuenfatueck became a PoW after he was shot down by fighters near Berlin on one of his first missions with the 352nd.

September 1944 saw a drastic change in the ground and air war in Europe. During the first few days of the new month, the Third Army's race across France began to slow up and eventually stop due to a shortage of fuel. The primary reason for this dilemma was that Gen George Patton's brilliant ground campaign had exceeded the expectations of even the most optimistic of Gen Eisenhower's planners.

D-Day plans stated that the armies would halt and regroup at the Seine River, before chasing the Germans deeper into their own territory. Since no one could have foreseen the Third Army's incredible breakthrough, these plans had to be abandoned in order to keep the Germans on the run, and thus prevent them from regrouping. The fuel crisis reached its peak on 5 September, however, and Patton's advance came to a halt.

In spite of the front now becoming static, VIII Fighter Command continued its strikes against German troops, transportation and facilities in occupied Europe, and its pilots dealt the retreating Wehrmacht some devastating blows. Hundreds of locomotives, trucks and aircraft were laid to waste in these attacks, but again 'the luck of the draw' resulted in the 352nd missing out on all of these attacks. On each of these missions the 'Bluenosers' ended up in quiet sectors, and came home empty-handed.

The mission of 8 September brought an end to the 352nd's inactivity when it travelled to Ludwigshafen, in Germany. After their arrival in the area, the 'Bluenosers' patrolled for 30 minutes before learning that the bombers had been recalled due to poor weather conditions. Ignoring the latter, Lt Col John Meyer decided to go down and locate some targets anyway. His intuition paid off as they arrived in the Heidelberg area.

Leaving the 486th FS 'upstairs' as top cover, Meyer led the 487th and 328th down to the deck. During the next 15 minutes the roving Mustangs raised hell with rail and highway traffic, destroying 20 locomotives and rail cars, seven trucks and a staff car, as well as damaging numerous other vehicles. The 328th made it through the attack without suffering any casualties, but the 487th was not so lucky. One of its senior pilots, Capt Duncan Donahue, was killed when the target he was strafing exploded in front of him – he had been with the unit since 1943. Also 'lost' was Flt Off Cyril Doleac, who landed in France on his way home when his Mustang suffered mechanical failure. Although initially posted as missing in action, Doleac actually spent some very enjoyable days relaxing in France while his fighter was being repaired, and he returned to Bodney soon thereafter.

When Cy Doleac received new P-51D-15 44-15383 in the autumn of 1944, he decided to do away with the *EX-LAX* nickname in favour of the more stylish *Maid of Orleans* – he was a native of New Orleans, Louisiana (*352nd FG Assocaition*)

Two more escort missions were flown on 9-10 September, and in both instances the Luftwaffe failed to make an appearance. After two straight days of this inactivity by enemy aircraft, John Meyer again decided to go down and find them.

The first airfield he planned to strafe was covered with dummy aircraft so Meyer headed on to Wertheim, where he found what he was looking for. After first neutralising the flak emplacements, Lt Col Meyer led his 487th FS in eight strafing runs across the airfield, and by the time the group had finished 20 aircraft had been engulfed in flames. Capt Clarence

A close-up view of the nose of Capt John Bennett's P-51D-5 44-13878. Note the stacks of crated drop tanks in the background (*352nd FG Association*)

Johnson showed the way with five destroyed (virtually all the aircraft shot up were Ju 52/3ms, with the remainder being unidentified transports), followed by Meyer with four, Lt Joe Ayers with three, Lts Malcolm Pickering and Phanor Waters with two each and Lts Jack Landrum, Dean Huston, Glenn Bowers and Alden Rigby with one apiece. All the 'Bluenosers' returned safely.

The Eighth Air Force selected industrial and petroleum facilities throughout Germany as its targets for 11 September, and its airmen found themselves facing the largest force deployed by the Luftwaffe since the spring of 1944. The 1st Air Task Force, which had been assigned targets in the Ruhrland, Behlen and Baux areas, was hit first, and its escort fighters dealt their opponents a resounding defeat. In three separate engagements three fighter groups claimed a total of 57 aerial victories, 14 of which were credited to the 'Bluenosers'.

The 328th FS was the first to score when Capt Bill Hendrian chased an Fw 190 to the deck before firing a fatal burst into the fleeing enemy fighter. The Focke-Wulf exploded upon hitting the ground. He then drove another Fw 190 off of Lt Richard Semon's tail, allowing the latter pilot to turn the tables on his quarry. After one burst from Semon's 'fifties', the Fw 190 bellied in and exploded.

The bulk of the victories claimed on this day fell to the 487th FS, which continued its butchery of the Luftwaffe with 12 aerial and four strafing kills. The squadron's leading scorer was none other than John Meyer, who in his most successful aerial combat to date downed three Bf 109s and one Fw 190. His fourth kill was achieved with only his right wing guns firing, and just 587 rounds were expended in downing this quartet of aircraft. With eight victories in two days, Lt Col John C Meyer had increased his total to 25.5 (12.5 of which were aerial kills), and he was now closing in on George Preddy as the group's leading ace.

Capt John Bennett followed Meyer down, and immediately after confirming his CO's first kill, turned to attack another Bf 109. He only succeeded in damaging it before the crippled aircraft vanished into a cloud bank. Then Bennett and his wingman, Lt Alden Rigby, climbed back to 5000 ft, and as they turned in the direction of the bomber stream, Bennett saw a Bf 109 settling in behind Rigby and warned him of the danger. For some reason the German did not open fire on Rigby, perhaps mistaking the olive drab-finished P-51B for a Bf 109, and this gave Capt Bennett the opportunity to attack. He scored numerous hits on the enemy aircraft before again losing his prey to 'Axis weather'.

As he and Rigby started to climb once more, an Fw 190 that was being pursued by a Mustang passed under him, and Bennett followed. The unidentified P-51 broke off its pursuit and Bennett bounced the fighter, downing it after a chase that took them as low as 50 ft above German soil.

Note the exceptionally light blue nose on Lt Bill Reese's P-51B 'PZ-R'. Photographed in the weeks immediately after D-Day, this machine was flown by Capt Donald Higgins during the first 'Shuttle Mission' to Russia (*352nd FG Association*)

The senior pilots of the 487th did not claim all the kills, however, for three of the enemy aircraft fell to Lt James Forga of Blue Flight, who had arrived at Bodney in June 1944. Blue Flight had caught about 30 Fw 190s in the landing pattern at Gottingen airfield, and Flight Leader Capt Clarence Johnson ordered the bounce. As Blue Flight was in its dive, one of the Fw 190s pulled up and attacked Forga, but the German failed to hit his target. This proved to be a fatal error, for the young Mustang pilot turned into him and shot him down with one burst from 100 yards.

As this aeroplane crashed, Lt Forga turned his attention to a second Fw 190 and quickly downed it too. His final kill was a Bf 109 that passed right in front of him as he pulled up from his previous victory. The remainder of Blue Flight clobbered four more aircraft, raising the 487th's total to 12 aerial victories for the day. Capt Johnson was credited with two Bf 109s, while Lts Duerr Schuh and Phanor Waters claimed a Bf 109 and an Fw 190 respectively – this was the first of five aerial kills for Schuh.

The squadron had still not finished, however, for Lts Henry Stewart, Ray Littge and Alex Sears also strafed two airfields, claiming another four Ju 88s destroyed and four damaged. Littge led the strafers with two destroyed and two damaged.

The 486th did not participate in the aerial combat on 11 September, but its pilots did strafe the Hertzburg railyards. Here, they destroyed two locomotives and a goods car, but Lt Howard Combs was shot down and killed by flak. The 328th also suffered one casualty in its air battle when Lt Garland Rayborn was shot down by fighters and became a PoW.

When the 352nd returned to Germany on the 12th it was met by another huge gaggle of German fighters, and the 'Bluenosers' again dealt with the enemy decisively.

Elements of the 328th and 486th FSs went into action almost simultaneously at a point north of Kyritz. The first of the German fighters fell to the 328th, with Lt John Stott downing an Fw 190 and Lts Charles

Cesky and James Lambright sharing another Focke-Wulf. Tempering this success was the loss of squadronmate Lt Joseph Broadwater, who some believe initiated the bounce and forced some of the enemy aircraft away from the bombers. He was shot down and killed during the action.

Now it was the 486th's turn, and within ten minutes its pilots had downed eight enemy aircraft and damaged a ninth. Lt Earl Lazear, White Flight Leader, claimed three Bf 109s for his first confirmed kills of the war, and he was now on the road to becoming an ace. His first two victims fell within seconds of each other, Lazear requiring just one well-placed burst per aircraft to shoot them down. Such modest force was not required for the Mustang pilot's third kill, Lazear chasing the enemy fighter down to the deck, where its pilot proceeded to lose control and crash.

Lt Bill Gerbe also scored his first kills of the war, and saved a buddy's life in the process. In this brief encounter, Gerbe downed two Bf 109s that had pulled into a firing position behind Lt Cecil Freeman. The latter pilot then added another Bf 109 to the mission tally after he had first managed to extricate himself from a swarm of enemy aircraft. As this fighter fell to earth, Lts Ernest Bostrom and Glen Wensch jumped in and sent two more down in flames, while Lt Tom Kyle damaged a third – this lucky German was the only survivor from his formation.

Fifteen minutes later the 486th found another gaggle of enemy aircraft, and three more German fighters crashed to earth. Capt Henry Miklajcyk downed one of them and shared a second with Lt Joseph Carter, while the final aerial kill of the day was claimed by Lt John Stearns. Not yet satisfied, Capt Miklajcyk (who had just 'made ace') dropped down and flamed a Ju 52/3m on Kustrin airfield as the squadron headed back to Bodney.

With 14 aircraft destroyed and two damaged claims on this mission, the 352nd finished this three-day period of action with a total of 55 destroyed and nine damaged, giving the group a spectacular kill ratio of 18.33-to-1.

Events in the ground war would soon change the 352nd's operations in mid-September. An airborne invasion of Holland, code-named Operation *Market-Garden*, was in the works, and the 'Bluenosers', along with the rest of VIII Fighter Command, would be supporting this assault.

The plan called for British and American paratroopers and glider assault units to make landings behind the German lines at the Dutch towns of Arnhem and Nijmegen, where they were to seize important bridges over rivers and canals. It was hoped that this daring assault would help break the stalemate, and give Allied ground forces a chance to kick start the stalled ground offensive. The airborne assault was planned for 17 September, and if vulnerable troop carriers and gliders were to have any chance of reaching the drop zone, German anti-aircraft positions in the target area would have to be destroyed. This 'flak-busting' mission fell to Allied fighters, with the Thunderbolt groups flying the bulk of the sorties. The Mustang groups of the Eighth Air Force were also called on to assist in this task, and they carried out their job admirably.

On 17 September the 352nd FG was divided into A and B groups. The first group was made up of the 328th and 486th FSs, and they would attack flak positions, while B Group, composed of 15 aircraft from the 487th FS, flew top cover. The 'Bluenosers' slid in beside the transports near the Belgian coastal town of Nieuwpoort and escorted them to the drop zones, where they were met by a veritable wall of light and heavy flak coming from a multitude of positions.

The attack flights of the 352nd immediately dived on the German gun positions, and before leaving, the 'Bluenosers' had destroyed four tanks, two half-tracks and six trucks, and killed approximately 35 German soldiers. The 352nd completed the mission with no losses, but the transports were not so lucky. Returning 352nd pilots reported the crash sites of at least 16 C-47s.

The 487th FS's Capt Robert K Butler poses with his P-51D-10 44-14785 *Channel Belle 2nd* 'HO-B'. Butler had the misfortune of being shot down by flak on D-Day whilst flying Bill Whisner's P-51B-10 42-106449 *Princess ELIZABETH*, although he successfully landed in Allied territory and went on to complete his tour in April 1945 (*352nd FG Association*)

During the next few days the 352nd flew a number of missions over the *Market-Garden* area, and one escort mission to Germany. All were uneventful and without loss of life, but the mission of 23 September brought this run of good fortune to an abrupt end.

When the 'Bluenosers' returned to Holland in support of the airborne troops on this day, they were first met by continuous and accurate anti-aircraft fire in the southern sector of the drop zone. First to fall was Maj Jack Blanchard of the 328th FS, whose Mustang was hit by flak near Gennup. He was seen parachuting from his aircraft and appeared to be okay – he evaded capture. Forty-five minutes later Red Flight of the 487th disappeared without a trace.

The flight, composed of Capt Clarence Johnson and Lts Phanor Waters, Joe Ayers and John Clark, was last seen near the Dutch town of Hengelo at 1700 hrs, and its last radio transmission was received 30 minutes later, the pilots giving their position as near Almelo, again in Holland. After this Red Flight vanished, and its disappearance remained a mystery until Lt John Clark was released from captivity and related the story.

In his account of the incident, Clark not only filled a void in the group's records, but corrected them as well. The mission summary for 23 September stated 'No enemy aircraft seen'. This may have been true for the remainder of the 352nd's pilots, but not for Red Flight. Clark remembered the incident as follows;

'We were flying the normal four abreast formation at about 1500 ft when we started to get a lot of fire from the ground. We then dropped down to 500 ft. Then we started to make a right circle, and we still had our drop tanks on. After nearly completing the circle, I looked to my right and up, and I caught a glimpse of about eight FW 190s just before they opened fire. They had spotted us just under the cloud cover that was about 8/10s at 600 to 700 ft.

'I pushed everything to the wall and started a sharp right turn and continued to turn right, but the '190 behind me continued to fire and he finally got inside of me. Then a burst caught me near the pilot's seat (right side) and continued on into the engine which caught fire. My P-51 was burning really good so I pulled the canopy release, disconnected my harness and just stood up and the wind pulled me out. I was lucky not to hit the tail – this is not a good way to get out of a P-51! I pulled the rip cord and the 'chute opened, and as I swung the first time I hit the ground.'

Ten minutes later Clark was captured, and this was probably a good thing since he had received a nasty leg wound that required immediate treatment. Lt Clark learned after reaching the Interrogation Centre in November that the remaining members of his flight had all been killed during the one-sided engagement.

Johnson, Ayers and Waters had been taken completely by surprise, and quickly shot down by the attacking Fw 190s from 5./JG 26. Leading the German formation was *Staffelführer* Leutnant Gerhard Vogt, who claimed two of the P-51s destroyed to boost his tally to 42 kills. Oberfelwebel Wilhelm Mayer was credited with a single victory to take his score to 21, while Fahnrich Maximilian Busch was killed when his Fw 190 collided with the fourth Mustang. Both Vogt and Mayer would subsequently lose their lives in combat flying the Fw 190D in early January 1945, Vogt having by then claimed 48 kills and Mayer 27.

Capt Johnson and Lts Ayer and Waters were buried near Calcar, in Germany.

Losing five aeroplanes and pilots on one mission was quite a blow to the 352nd, and the incident sent shock waves through the 487th FS. This engagement was the worst single defeat suffered by the squadron at the hands of German fighters during the entire war. The flight leader, Capt Clarence 'Tuffy' Johnson, was one of the 352nd's rising stars, having joined the group in mid-August 1944 after completing two combat tours in the P-38 (with the 96th FS/82nd FG in the MTO and then the 436th FS/479th FG in the ETO). Johnson had also claimed five aerial kills with the Lightning, and had already added two Bf 109s shot down and five Ju 52/3ms and an He 177 destroyed on the ground to his tally during his brief spell time with the 487th FS.

The luckiest pilot on this ill-fated 23 September mission was Lt Elmer Smith of the 328th FS, whose Mustang took a hit from an 88 mm shell in its right wing. The round missed Smith's ammunition box by only a quarter of an inch, and left a three-foot hole in the wing. The pilot, who had already miraculously survived the North Sea 'incident' (on 21 July 1944)

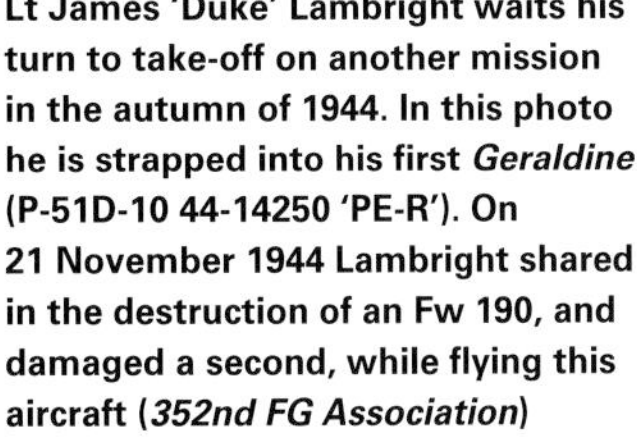

Lt James 'Duke' Lambright waits his turn to take-off on another mission in the autumn of 1944. In this photo he is strapped into his first *Geraldine* (P-51D-10 44-14250 'PE-R'). On 21 November 1944 Lambright shared in the destruction of an Fw 190, and damaged a second, while flying this aircraft (*352nd FG Association*)

P-51D-5 44-13688 *"DONNA DAE" VI* was the sixth aircraft assigned to Lt Leo Northrup, all of which he named after his favourite Hollywood actress. This fighter enjoyed only a brief life in the frontline with the 486th FS, for it suffered mechanical failure over the German island of Heligoland, in the North Sea, on 27 August and its pilot, Lt Charles Ferris, was forced to bail out. Ferris was not recovered (*352nd FG Association*)

by nursing his fuel-starved P-51 back to England, again proved his skill by bringing his mangled Mustang safely back to Bodney.

Two escort missions were flown on 27 September, and the first one found Yellow Flight of the 328th FS mixing it up with a large gaggle of Bf 109s and Fw 190s near Frankfurt. Shortly after receiving an alert from the 487th FS that many enemy aircraft had been seen in the area, Capt Don Bryan spotted a huge formation of 100-150 fighters passing over his flight. He climbed after them, and Flt Off William Montgomery's report relates what followed;

'Yellow Leader (Capt Bryan) climbed above them and we attacked as they hit the bombers. There were only three of us in Yellow Flight, and Yellow Three, Lt Richard Brookins, was unable to stay with us as we climbed with full throttle and full RPM. Capt Bryan singled out an Me-109 and opened fire. The enemy aircraft immediately burst into flames. Bryan then opened fire on another Me-109 that was nearby, and it also burst into flames and fell away in a spin.

'At this point I lost Capt Bryan as I tried to open fire on the enemy aircraft, but my guns would not fire. After checking my gun-switch, I made several more attempts to open fire, but my guns would not fire. I immediately broke left to get out of the combat area, and as I did so, I pulled in behind a '109 that was also in a steep left turn. The enemy pilot saw me and tried to steepen his turn, but as he did so, he stalled and snapped over on his back and went into a spin at approximately 21,000 ft. I went over the top of him, and could not see him for a short time. As soon as I could clear myself, I pulled out to one side and observed a '109 that was in a vicious spin. It broke into the clouds at about 2000 ft. I learned later from Lt Brookins that the pilot bailed out.'

In the meantime, Lt Brookins had found himself alone in the midst of a gaggle of German fighters;

'Capt Bryan and F/O Montgomery had left me behind by about a half-mile to one mile. As they reached and attacked the box of '109s, I saw another box of about 60 FW 190s and Me-109s above me. There was no support behind me, and being alone, I turned up and into them. I was too busy to fire as I went through them. Most of them spread out, some split-essing and others climbing.

'As I passed them I rolled over on my back and followed an FW 190 down. I closed fast and gave him a short burst from 200-100 yards. The enemy aircraft exploded in flames and broke up into several pieces. The enemy pilot managed to bail out and I saw his 'chute open at 16,000 ft.'

Capt Don Bryan finished off his day by damaging another Bf 109 before leading his flight back to Bodney, these victories taking his tally of aerial kills to 6.333. They also closed out the 352nd FG's scoring for the month of September 1944.

THE LULL AND THEN THE STORM

October 1944 saw a re-organisation take place within the Eighth Air Force. A major aspect of these changes was the order relieving VIII Fighter Command of operational control of its 15 fighter groups. Under the new plan, these units would report directly to the Bomber Divisions. The three Fighter Wings, the 65th, 66th and 67th, now reported, respectively, to the 2nd, 3rd and 1st Divisions (the 352nd would now report to the latter division). The reasoning behind the changes was that the new system would simplify the chain of command, thus making it easier to plan the escort requirements for each mission.

Another noticeable change in October was the absence of the Luftwaffe. After suffering heavy losses of aeroplanes and pilots during September, the German High Command had apparently decided to hoard its remaining forces and try to rebuild its shattered fighter units. The long lull in action was noted in the 352nd FG's War Diary;

'October 1944 was probably the most uneventful operational month in the history of the 352nd FG. Because of generally adverse weather conditions only 15 missions were flown, most of which could be described as milk runs.'

Second from the left in this photograph of pilots from the 487th FS is Texan Lt Jack Landrum, whose death in action on 24 October 1944 inspired Chaplain George Cameron to begin his campaign of presenting $1000.00 War Bonds to the children of 352nd FG pilots killed in combat (*352nd FG Association*)

Lt Landrum was flying this P-51D-5 on the day he was shot down by light flak whilst strafing targets near Hannover. He had inherited the Mustang from squadronmate Lt William 'Flaps' Fowler when the latter pilot had completed his tour in September 1944. It is seen here whilst still assigned to Fowler, and it features his *STARDUST* nickname and four kill symbols for his 2.5 aerial victories and one strafing kill. Landrum renamed the machine *Moose* (*352nd FG Association*)

The lack of aerial combat, however, did not eliminate losses in the 352nd, for three pilots were killed and three others ended up as PoWs during the month. The first to fall was Capt John Coleman of the 328th FS, whose Mustang suffered mechanical failure near the Dutch town of Tilburg on 5 October. Crash-landing his fighter, Coleman succeeded in evading capture and returning to Allied territory. The following day mechanical maladies struck again when the 487th's Lt James Forga experienced a loss of power in his P-51B over the German island of Wangerooge. Despite Forga being seen to bail out, he was posted Missing in Action – this was later changed to Killed in Action.

A further two losses occurred on 24 October during strafing attacks in Germany. The first pilot lost was Lt Thompson R Kyle of the 486th, who bailed out of his flak damaged P-51B over Hannover and subsequently became a PoW. Young Texan Lt Jack Landrum of the 487th was not so lucky, his P-51D being hammered by light flak during a strafing run over Wildeshausen, causing the pilot to crash to his death.

The loss of Lt Jack Landrum touched Bodney's Chaplain (Capt) George Cameron, and compelled him to see if something could be done in Landrum's memory. His decision was to encourage the 'Bluenosers' to lend a hand to his young family, and they responded by presenting a $1000.00 War Bond to Jack Landrum's infant son, Bob. The response to Chaplain Cameron's appeal was so generous that he continued his efforts, and by war's end a number of $1000.00 War Bonds had been presented to the children of pilots who died in the service of their country.

An interesting postscript to this story occurred after the 352nd FG Association was formed during the 1980s. The Association decided to see if any of the 'War Bond' children could be located, and its search was

Parked in the middle of 'frozen fog' at Bodney late in 1944, 'PZ-N' of the 486th FS is prepared for its next mission by a lone groundcrewman. Note the 'gas wagon' trundling along the taxyway (*352nd FG Association*)

successful. Bob Landrum was tracked down, and he faithfully attended the reunions of the 352nd FG Association until they ended in September 2000.

On 1 November 1944 Lt Bill Gerbe of the 486th FS became the first 'Bluenoser' to participate in the downing of an Me 262. He was flying his assigned P-51D-10 44-14087 *LITTLE GYP* ('PZ-Z') on this occasion. Given a shared credit in its destruction, the Me 262 took Lt Gerbe's total of aerial victories to 2.5 – these are all marked with kill symbols below the windscreen. Gerbe, who flew 76 missions between August 1944 and April 1945, would add no further air or ground claims to his tally (*Marc Hamel*)

As October drew to a close, many of the 352nd FG's veteran pilots returned to Bodney after completing their 30-day leaves in the US. The roster of pilots beginning their second tour of duty with the 352nd included Col Joe Mason, Lt Col Willie O Jackson, Maj George Preddy and Capt Ed Heller. The return of leading ace George Preddy to the 487th FS was to be short-lived, however, for on 28 October he took over command of the 328th FS from Lt Col John C Edwards.

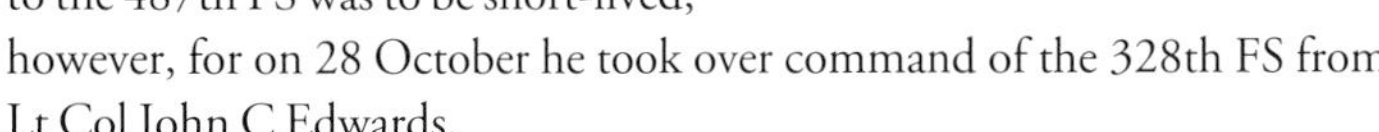

By November 1944 it was beginning to appear that the Luftwaffe was finished as an effective defender against the Allied Air Forces' aerial onslaught. Eighth Air Force fighters had reported virtually no encounters with enemy aircraft during the last two weeks of October, and the 352nd had not scored an aerial victory since 27 September.

Logic would have supported this argument since the German fighter forces had been decimated during the first nine months of the year, but in this case, things were far different to how they appeared. Allied intelligence knew that German aircraft production had increased in spite of the continual bombing of its production facilities, and that it was probably only a matter of time before a rebuilt Luftwaffe fighter force would reappear en masse over Germany.

The mission of 1 November promised to be yet another uneventful trip to Germany for the 'Bluenosers'. However, as the group turned round and started its return flight to Bodney, a mixed force of Me 163s and Me 262s appeared in its flightpath. The first enemy aircraft to attempt an interception was a rocket-powered Me 163, and its incredible performance (maximum speed of 596 mph) easily carried it away from the pursuing 486th FS Mustangs, but the Me 262 which appeared a few minutes later was not as fortunate.

The German pilot was attempting to lure White Flight of the 486th away from the bombers, and he failed to see Capt Chet Harker's Red Flight closing in on him until it was too late. Moments later Lt William T Gerbe became the first 'Bluenoser' to share in the destruction of an Me 262. His combat report stated;

'We first saw this Me 262 at our altitude, which was 31,000 ft. He made a pass on the flight in front of us and started a diving turn to the right. At about 12,000 or 13,000 ft, Red Flight was closing in on him. I had more speed than my element leader so I called on the R/T and told him I was going after the Jerry. Just about that time the Me 262 made a turn into me. I turned with him and it put me right on his tail. I was using the K-14 gunsight, and first opened fire at 200 yards, saw hits on the tail section, closed to about 150 yards and shot out his right engine as he was climbing

This is a still from Lt Gerbe's camera gun film of his attack on an Me 262 over Arnhem-Hengelo, in Holland, on 1 November 1944. He shared in its demise with a P-47 pilot from the 56th FG. A Thunderbolt from this group can indeed be seen in the background of this still (*352nd FG Association*)

to leave me behind. After I shot his right jet out the Me 262 went into a flat spin to the right. The pilot bailed out a few seconds later.

'While the aeroplane was spinning down about 16+ P-51s and P-47s were taking shots at it. The Me 262 did not catch fire. The pilot bailed out at about 9000 ft. My Flight Leader, Capt Harker, had been able to close to within firing range of the enemy aircraft when he made the 180-degree turn. He fired several bursts and I observed strikes in the tail section. When the enemy aircraft pulled up into a climb, Capt Harker followed him, but I was in a better position to close to a shorter range.

'I claim one Me 262 destroyed, shared with Capt Harker.'

As it turned out Capt Harker's claim was disallowed, and Lt Walter Groce of the P-47-equipped 63rd FS/56th FG was given credit for sharing in the victory. This kill was the only claim made by Eighth Air Force fighters on 1 November, and this mission gave no clue as to what would occur the following day.

The target for 2 November was a familiar one – the petroleum refineries in and around Merseburg. In an all out attempt to destroy these often bombed facilities, the Eighth Air Force despatched a massive force of 1100 bombers and nearly 900 fighters to carry out the task. Knowing that these targets would more than likely be well defended, mission planners laid out an erratic routing for its strike force in the hope that it would disguise the bombers' true objectives. German controllers were not fooled by this plan, however, and concentrated at least ten *gruppen* over the target area. At approximately 1200 hrs these forces met, and one of the largest air battles of World War 2 commenced.

The 3rd Air Division was struck first, and its escort fighters downed 19 enemy aircraft in the opening engagements. Twenty minutes later it was the 1st Air Division's turn to do battle with a huge force of enemy

Capt Donald S Bryan of the 328th FS poses with his P-51D-10 44-14061 *Little One III* after his big day on 2 November 1944 when he shot down five Bf 109s near Merseburg (*via William N Hess*)

aircraft. As the German fighters began to close on the B-17s, their movements were watched by 328th FS CO Maj George Preddy. Moments after he reported spotting this formation of 50 enemy aircraft, other gaggles of German fighters were seen moving into the area, so the three 'Bluenose' squadrons split up and chose their respective targets.

The 328th FS charged into one of the gaggles, and within 15 to 20 minutes Preddy's pilots had downed an astounding 25 Bf 109s – a new Eighth Air Force record for victories by a squadron in a single mission. Capt Don Bryan led the way with five kills (and two damaged), and close behind him were Lt Arthur Hudson with four and Capt William J Stangel and Lt Charles Goodman with three apiece. Three pilots, Maj Earl Abbott and Lts Charles Rogers and Glenn Clark, scored doubles, and the remaining four enemy aircraft were claimed by Maj George Preddy and Lts Eugene James, Francis Hill and DeWayne Maxwell.

Don Bryan, already an ace with 6.33 kills, nearly doubled his score on this mission, and he described his big day in a detailed encounter report;

'I was leading Yellow Flight with Lts Hill, Montgomery and Briggs as my Nos 2, 3 and 4 men respectively. I was flying at about 28,000 ft. Just before reaching the target, many contrails were called in coming from the east. I turned on my switches and

When Maj Preddy became CO of the 328th FS, he received this P-51D-15 44-14906 'PE-P'. His crew chief, Art Snyder, applied all of Preddy's personal markings on the left side, and then, with the major's permission, added his barber's pole on the right (*352nd FG Association*)

prepared for combat. Shortly after that I saw the contrails, and was able to identify them as Me 109s. There seemed to be about 50 of them – approximately 40 in a box, with several more above as top cover. By the time I could get into position for my bounce about 10-15 of them had started down on the bombers – the others were preparing to start down. I figured that if I hit the middle of them I could break up the attack.

'I led my flight in a diving attack into the midst of the enemy aircraft. I closed to about 100 yards on one of the Me 109s. Using the K-14 sight for the first time, I got only a few strikes. I overran this enemy aircraft by diving under him about 20 ft. As I did so I looked back and saw that his cooling system was shot out. I claim this enemy aircraft damaged.

'My number 3 man called and said there was an enemy aircraft positioning itself on me. I did a snap roll and lost the Me 109 very effectively, plus the rest of my own flight.

'For the next ten minutes I was in at least 15 separate combats. During this time I made a stern attack on enemy aircraft flying in string (one behind the other). I attacked the last enemy aircraft in the string and observed many strikes. This Me 109 went down in flames. I claim this enemy aircraft destroyed.

'There were many other formations of enemy aircraft in the immediate vicinity. I then proceeded to attack another Me 109 from astern and got many good hits on the fuselage and wings. Many pieces flew off and the enemy aircraft began to emit much black smoke and started down from about 10,000 ft. I last observed this enemy aircraft in a steep dive going through the undercast at 4000 ft with a great deal of smoke pouring from it. I claim this enemy aircraft as destroyed. During the melee I attacked another Me 109, getting strikes. I claim this aircraft damaged. While I was making these attacks I was being constantly engaged by other Me 109s.

'I then saw a single Me 109 and a P-51, which I later learned was being flown by Lt (Milton) Camerer of my squadron. These two aircraft were in

Capt William J Stangel poses with his P-51D-5 44-14015 *Stinky 2* after downing three Bf 109s near Merseburg on 2 November 1944. He subsequently 'made ace' with two more Bf 109 victories on Christmas Day (*William J Stangel*)

This photo provides a good view of Lt Fred A Cast's unusually decorated trim tab and upper rudder hinge on his *Eileen I*, alias P-51D-5 44-13553 'PE-U'. Cast inherited this aircraft from Lt Ed Zellner, who was shot down in another D-5 on 31 July 1944 (*352nd FG Association*)

an engagement, bobbing in and out of the clouds. I attacked the enemy aircraft, which dove into the clouds at about 4000 ft. This Me 109 came out of the clouds shortly after that, and I made several attacks on him as he went in and out of the clouds.

'After several attacks, I was able to make what I thought was going to be a head-on pass – as it turned out I was at about 90 degrees to the enemy aircraft. I opened fire at about 500 yards and closed to about 150 yards, observing strikes in the cockpit and on the wing. This enemy aircraft nosed over sharply and went down through the undercast, with gas pouring from his wing root. I followed him down and observed him in a very steep dive towards the ground at about 1000 ft, indicating about 350 or 400 mph. I later learned from Lt Camerer, who had joined me and was flying on my wing, that this Me 109 crashed and exploded. I claim this enemy aircraft destroyed.

'I then started back up toward the bombers, with Lt Camerer on my wing. At about 10,000 ft I observed two Me 109s (F or G) flying just above the undercast at 5000 ft. I moved into position and split-essed onto the last one. I had only two guns firing as I made my attack. At about 500 yards I opened fire and hit the enemy aircraft very hard around the fuselage and wings. At about 300 yards I hit it on the wing, and either the wing-tip or the top of the wing flew off. The enemy aircraft snapped into a very violent spin to the left and spun through the undercast in flames. I claim this enemy aircraft destroyed.

'I proceeded to attack the lead ship of the formation then, and got strikes on him. One of my guns stopped firing at this time, so I had only one gun firing, and it threw me off a bit. I found it difficult to get many strikes while closing from 350 to 150 yards. When I closed to about 80 yards I got strikes through the fuselage and wing roots. I broke off the attack and the enemy aircraft went through the undercast at 4000 ft in a very steep dive, indicating about 350 mph, with much black smoke pouring from it. I claim this enemy aircraft destroyed. I then climbed back to altitude and returned to base without further incident.

'I claim 5 enemy aircraft destroyed and 2 enemy aircraft damaged (air).'

The remaining 13 victories for the day were claimed by the 486th and 487th FSs. Two 'Bluenosers', Capt Henry Miklajcyk of the 486th FS and Lt Glenn Clark of the 328th FS, were lost during the engagement, both of whom were shot down. 'Hank' Miklajcyk, who had been with the group since 28 December 1942, and who had scored 13 kills (7.5 of which were aerial victories), was killed after he had downed a Bf 109 and an Fw 190. Clark (with three aerial victories) became a PoW.

After losing an astounding 134 aircraft on 2 November to Allied fighters, the Luftwaffe again went into hiding for several days. During this lull in activity the 352nd FG underwent some changes in command. Col Joe Mason completed his tour of duty and was replaced by Col James Mayden as Group Commander, while Lt Col John C Meyer was named Deputy Group Commander and Maj William T Halton given command of the 487th FS.

On 9 November the recent spate of mechanical failures that had plagued the 352nd continued when Lt Charles Rogers (who had claimed two victories exactly one week earlier) of the 328th FS was killed when an engine problem brought his P-51D down north-east of Lille.

Col James D Mayden's second *StrawBoss* enjoyed a far longer life than his first machine (see page 77). As this photograph illustrates, crew chief Hubert Robling kept P-51D-10 44-14111 'PE-X' in an immaculate condition. It is seen here parked on its hardstanding at Bodney in the late autumn of 1944. Note the hammock slung between two poles in the background! (*352nd FG Association*)

The Eighth Air Force paid a return visit to the petroleum facilities around Merseburg on 21 November with a force of 700 bombers and 650 fighters. As the massive attack force moved into Germany, they found a huge cloud cover between them and the target. The weather front was so bad that the German controllers thought the mission would be recalled, and therefore did not scramble their fighters until it was too late.

On this mission the 352nd FG was split into A and B Groups, each with a slightly different assignment. A Group (the 328th FS), which remained with the bombers, encountered enemy aircraft just before reaching the target area. In two separate engagements over a 30-minute period, the 328th destroyed 7.5 Fw 190s and damaged several others. Meanwhile, B Group was on a freelance sweep when it encountered a formation of 50+ Fw 190s, with another large gaggle positioned as top cover, near Leipzig.

Senior men in the 352nd FG get together for a group shot at Bodney in early November 1944. They are, from left to right, Lt Col James Mayden (soon to become CO of the group), Maj Willie O Jackson (CO of the 486th FS), Maj George Preddy (CO of the 328th FS), Col Joe Mason (then CO of the group) and Lt Col John Meyer (CO of the 487th FS and soon to become Deputy CO of the group). They are posing in front of 'Red Dog' Mason's P-51D-15 44-14911 *THIS IS IT!* ('PZ-M'), which was the last of six fighters (two P-47Ds, two P-51Bs and two P-51Ds) that had been assigned to him during his ETO tour. Note the 487th FS badge on 'J C' Meyer's A2 flying jacket (*via Michael O'Leary*)

The German flightpath paralleled the bombers' withdrawal route, and it was obvious they were planning an immediate attack.

The spearhead of B Group was a flight of eight Mustangs of the 487th FS, led by Lt Col J C Meyer. Realising the enemy's intentions Meyer led his flight after them and shattered the German formation. By the time his spearhead had finished, 12 enemy aircraft had been shot out of the sky. Leading the decimation was Capt Bill Whisner with five destroyed and two probables, followed by John Meyer with three kills and Lts Karl Waldron and Nelson Jessup with two apiece.

Overall, the 'Bluenosers' had claimed a total of 19.5 destroyed, two probables and six damaged without the loss of any of its own pilots. For his extraordinary heroism on this mission, Capt William T Whisner was awarded the DSC. His overall tally of aerial kills now stood at 9.5.

The next few missions were relatively quiet, but on 27 November German fighters again challenged the 352nd FG. A further 18 Bf 109s were claimed destroyed (and one damaged) in the ensuing dogfight, with the 487th FS leading the way with 15 victories. The squadron diary summed the battle up well;

'On 27 November the Me 109s came up with a vengeance to bounce our boys, but when they bounced back to Göring, 16 of them were missing, being on our victory board instead.'

Capt Walter Starck downed three, Capts Bill Whisner and Ralph Hamilton each scored doubles, and single victories were credited to Lt Col Meyer, Majs Bill Halton and Earl Duncan and Lts Sanford Moats, Karl Dittmer, Henry Stewart, Alden Rigby, Dean Huston and Ray Littge. The unit did not emerge from the dogfight unscathed, however, with newly-crowned ace Walter Starck (on what was supposed to be his 107th, and last, mission of his tour) being forced to bail out when the tail section of his third victim separated and struck his P-51D. The oil and coolant lines ruptured and the fighter's engine quickly overheated and burst into flames. Starck was soon captured, as was his squadronmate Capt Walter

Capt Bill Whisner and P-51D-10 44-14237 *Moonbeam McSWINE* forged a deadly partnership, claiming 12 aerial kills between 2 November 1944 and 1 January 1945. The 19 crosses on the fighter's fuselage also include Whisner's three strafing kills. Its nose has been freshly repainted in the late war darker shade of blue, and a close look at the photo shows the portion of the blue bearing the name has been left in the original shade (*via William N Hess*)

Upon his return from the big air battle of 21 November 1944, Capt Bill Whisner indicates his six victories scored that day. This gesture proved to be a little premature, as his score for the mission was later revised to five confirmed kills and one probable (*via William N Hess*)

Lt Karl Dittmer runs up his engine in preparation for a mission from Asch (Y-29), in Belgium. Note his crew chief in the background awaiting *DOPEY OKIE's* take-off. This photo shows that the nose of this P-51D-15 had also been repainted in the darker shade of blue, but that the panel bearing the name was left in the early shade (*352nd FG Association*)

Lt Karl Waldron and his P-51D-15 44-15513 *GOLIATH* are seen at Bodney in April 1945. The ten swastikas indicate Lt Waldron's final wartime tally of three aerial and seven strafing victories. Waldron damaged an Me 262 while flying this aircraft on 10 April 1945 (*352nd Fighter Group Association*)

Smith, who took to his parachute when the wing sheared off of his P-51 near Münster whilst diving after an enemy fighter.

The remaining victories of the day were credited to Lts Arthur Hudson and Charles Cesky of the 328th FS, the solitary kill for the latter pilot giving him ace status. After the battle had ended, a handful of men from the 328th went down to strafe targets of opportunity, and it was then that Lt Hudson was shot down and killed while strafing a German airfield at Aulendorf.

Combat operations for November were closed out with an escort mission to Böhlen on the last day of the month. Nearing Chemnitz, 10+ Bf 109s were spotted as they attempted to attack the bombers. The 486th FS, led by Lt Col Willie O Jackson, broke up the attack and shot down three of the Messerschmitts during the brief engagement. The Bf 109s were destroyed by Jackson and Lts Earl Lazear and Charles Griffiths. This single kill made 'Willie O' an ace.

November 1944 had been one of the 352nd FG's most successful months of the war. Its pilots had downed 80 aircraft in aerial combat and claimed many more probably destroyed or damaged in only 16 missions.

During the first eight days of December 1944 the 352nd FG flew virtually unopposed on its missions. On the 9th the targets were airfields and railyards near Stuttgart, and this time a handful of Me 262s rose to engage the bomber stream. One of the German pilots tried to bounce the 486th FS and paid for his mistake. Lt Harry Edwards saw the jet's approach, slid in behind it and opened fire. His first burst damaged the fighter's right engine, and the Me 262 tried to dive away. Edwards followed him down to 500 ft and destroyed the Messerschmitt's left

The 352nd FG's most successful 'train-buster' was the 486th FS's Lt Bruno Grabovski, who was credited with the destruction of more than 40 locomotives. His P-51B-10 (42-106439 *DUCHESS*) was coded 'PZ-Q', and had previously been assigned to Lt Martin Corcoran until he returned to the US in August 1944. Whilst flown by Corcoran, the fighter had been named *Button Nose*, and coded 'PZ-L' (*352nd FG Association*)

engine with a burst from 300 yards. He then closed to 50 yards, fired one final burst and watched the Me 262 crash and explode.

With this victory Lt Edwards became the first 'Bluenoser' to score a solo kill over an Me 262. On the way home he and his wingman, Lt Bruno Grabovski, did a little 'train-busting', the latter pilot being the group's specialist in 'train-busting'. He duly chalked up six more trains to his personal scoreboard, while Lt Edwards clobbered five goods wagons and one German soldier before they headed home.

During the next several days the weather over Europe became progressively worse, and flying in it was becoming dangerous. On the ground the soldiers were suffering from the brutal cold, and the 'Bluenosers' were only too glad to answer an appeal to donate extra blankets and shoes for them. It never would have occurred to the men of 352nd FG at this point in time that they too would soon be enduring this bone-chilling weather.

The severe winter snow storms that had seriously hampered Allied ground and aerial operations in western Europe were exactly what Hitler and his generals were praying for. Under the cover of the weather, Field Marshal Gerd von Rundstedt was massing thousands of troops in preparation for his counter-attack in the Ardennes Forest. On 17 December 1944 his troops smashed through Allied lines in Belgium and Luxembourg, and urgent requests went out from embattled GIs on the ground for close air support. However, weather conditions in the Ardennes area nullified aerial operations.

Knowing that air support, for the moment at least, was unavailable, Gen Eisenhower consulted with his generals, and approved George Patton's plan for stopping the German assault. Patton turned his Third Army around and marched 125 miles in two days to assist in the defence of Bastogne. As the battle on the ground was taking shape, an urgent call went out to send fighter groups to the frontlines, and on 22 December the 352nd was alerted for its move to Asch (Y-29), in Belgium.

While its pilots were on an escort mission to Germany, the 352nd's ground personnel required in Belgium were packing their equipment and loading it onto the waiting C-47s. The pilots had also stuffed as much cold weather gear into their Mustangs as possible because they would be landing at Asch when the mission was completed. By the end of the day all 352nd personnel had arrived in Belgium, and the 'Bluenosers' declared themselves ready to continue the war from Y-29.

The skies over Europe began to clear on 23 December, and the Eighth Air Force took full advantage of the flying weather. Over 1100 tons of bombs were dropped on marshalling yards, communications centres and railway lines supporting the German offensive. Aerial combat also resumed in a big way when Allied fighters downed 69 aircraft, probably destroyed one and damaged eight during the course of the day. The 328th FS joined in the action near Liège, in Belgium, with Capt Don Bryan and Lt William H Sanford each destroying an Fw 190.

Christmas Day 1944 saw no break in the fighting, and the engagements on the ground and in the air were ferocious. The German assault on Bastogne resumed that day in spite of the terrible punishment its forces had received from aerial bombing and artillery fire during the previous 24 hours. As Gen Tony McAuliffe's 101st Airborne Division continued to stubbornly defend its tiny perimeter in Belgium, the heavy bombers of the Eighth Air Force renewed their harassment of German supply lines.

The attacks on communication centres and rail lines west of the Rhine River drew the Luftwaffe out of hiding and into the air in an attempt to protect these critical facilities. Engagements with enemy aircraft were frequent, and eight of the twelve Eighth Air Force fighter groups operating in the area participated in the destruction of 46 German aircraft. The 328th FS played a major role in the day's air battles by shooting down 11 enemy fighters, but the squadron's great victory was totally overshadowed by the loss of its leader.

The 328th FS, led by Maj George Preddy, was on patrol when the controller vectored it toward enemy aircraft detected in the Koblenz area. South-west of the city two flights of Bf 109s, each numbering about 20, were spotted. As the second gaggle of enemy aircraft passed under Preddy's White Flight, he led three other members of the flight down to attack, and Capt Bill Stangel, flying as White 5, single-handedly bounced the first flight. Stangel subsequently reported;

Capt Bill Stangel and his wingman head down the runway at Chievres (Y-84), in Belgium, on an early April 1945 mission to Germany. P-51D-5 44-13815 *Stinky 2* ('PE-C') was used by Stangel to score all five of his kills. Quite why the fighter features six victory symbols remains a mystery, for Stangel submitted no claims for probables or strafing kills. Note that although Stangel's Mustang is devoid of underfuselage stripes, his wingman's is not (*352nd FG Association*)

'As I was No 5, I went into the first bunch alone and singled out an Me 109, giving him a short burst. He split-essed, I followed, he jettisoned his canopy and I gave him another short burst just as he bailed out at about 6000 ft. The enemy aircraft hit the ground and exploded.

Capt Charles Cesky poses with his new P-51D-5 44-13927 *Diann Ruth II* soon after the fighter's name had been applied (*Charles Cesky*)

'I turned away and shortly afterwards engaged another Me 109 at about 7500 ft. We started turning, and every once in a while I would take a short burst at him even though the deflection was great. I then gave him another short burst from the high starboard side and he went into a short dive. I followed, he then pulled up sharply, and he must have closed his power because I overshot him. I came around him and he bailed out as I was coming in for this pass. I passed just below him and circled until he hit the deck. The enemy aircraft crashed into a wood and exploded.'

While Capt Stangel was engaged in his one-man show (which took his score to five kills exactly), the remainder of White Flight was taking an additional toll of enemy aircraft. Maj Preddy shot down two Bf 109s for his 26th and 27th (26.83) aerial victories, and three more of the Messerschmitt fighters were knocked out of the sky by Lts James Lambright, Ray Mitchell and Charles Goodman, giving White Flight a total of seven kills in this engagement.

Blue Flight tried to join the fray at Koblenz but ran into the overcast and got separated. When they could not locate the rest of the flight, Capt Charles Cesky and his wingman, Lt Al Chesser, started back to Asch. As they approached the city of Maastricht, Cesky noticed a flight of four Fw 190s flying some 500 ft above them and he attacked. His first target was the number three aircraft, and the pilot bailed out as soon as Cesky's bullets slammed into his Fw 190. Then in quick succession Cesky shot

A full view of Capt Cesky's *Diann Ruth II* as she appeared at Asch during December 1944. Cesky claimed a trio of Fw 190s with this machine on Christmas Day, taking his final tally to 8.5 aerial kills (*Charles Cesky*)

Lt Gordon Cartee was George Preddy's wingman on 25 December 1944, and it was he who reported the tragic loss of the group's 'ace of aces'. Cartee's Mustang (P-51K-5 44-11560 'PE-C') was named *Steph'n Jane* on the left side and *Bonny* on the right side (*352nd FG Association*)

down the number two fighter and then the German flight leader. As Capt Cesky's victims tumbled from the sky, Lt Chesser shot the fourth Fw 190 down in flames. Cesky had boosted his final tally to 8.5 aerial kills with this trio of victories.

These four Fw 190s claimed by the 328th FS had raised the group's total for the day to eleven, but the event that was now about to unfold rocked the 352nd to its foundations.

As White Flight departed Koblenz the controller vectored it toward Liège to look for some low flying enemy aircraft that had been reported in the area. As Maj Preddy and his wingman, Lt Gordon Cartee, headed for Liège, they were joined by Lt James Bouchier of the 479th FG. As they approached the city, they were warned by R/T of intense flak, but the voice said it would be lifted when they got there.

South-west of Liège Maj Preddy observed a low flying Fw 190 and chased it at tree-top level into an area guarded by the US Army's 12th Anti-aircraft Group. The three Mustangs flew into a murderous flak barrage and Lt Cartee reported the tragedy that followed;

'As we went over the woods I was hit by ground fire. Maj Preddy apparently noticed the intense ground fire and light flak and we broke off the attack with a chandelle to the left. About half way through the manoeuvre, and at an altitude of about 700 ft, his canopy came off and he nosed down, still in his turn. I saw no 'chute and watched his ship hit.'

Gordon Cartee managed to get out of the area after seeing Maj Preddy crash, but Lt Bouchier was not so lucky. His Mustang was also hit by numerous 40 mm flak rounds and he bailed out. Bouchier made it down safely, but George Preddy was found dead in the wreckage of his P-51D. American guns had accidentally taken the life of one of America's finest fighter pilots, and the leading USAAF Mustang ace.

Back at Y-29 the men had just finished a wonderful Christmas dinner when the news of Maj Preddy's death was announced. The 'Bluenosers' were stunned, and Sgt Iggy Marinello noted in his diary, 'That news quickly brought home the ugly realities of war and did subdue the planned festivities'.

Back at Bodney some of the 487th FS personnel were in the NCO club enjoying a few beers when the 'bomb' was dropped. Joseph 'Red' McVay, who had served for many months as Preddy's assistant crew chief in the 487th FS, recalled;

'A silence came over the group. This could not happen, should not happen, could not be true. Not to Maj Preddy, the favourite of the 487th enlisted men. No one spoke. One by one they got up and left the area, left

When future 10.5-kill aerial ace Lt Raymond Littge received his first P-51D-5 (44-11330 'HO-M') in October 1944, he named it *E Pluribus Unum*. He scored eight of his victories in this aircraft, using it until February 1945 when it was damaged in a landing accident (*352nd FG Association*)

the keg of beer, to find some place where they could compose themselves and try to understand what had happened to their hero.'

On the ground, the heroic stand by the 101st Airborne Division at Bastogne had blunted the German offensive. The fighting would continue for several more days, but the momentum had now shifted to the Allies. The 352nd FG continued its coverage of the front, and on 26 December picked up where it had left off the day before by scoring another 13.5 kills during two engagements with the Luftwaffe.

The first fight of the day occurred at 0940 hrs when the 487th FS, led by Lt Col John Meyer, received a vector to Ollheim. The squadron arrived at the scene just in time to prevent two gaggles of Bf 109s from bouncing Ninth Air Force Thunderbolts that were dive-bombing German positions. Meyer led Red and White Flights in an attack against the leading enemy formation and sent Blue and Yellow Flights against the second gaggle, which was flying top cover.

First blood was drawn by Maj Bill Halton's Yellow Flight, which quickly downed two Bf 109s. The first of these fell to Lt Walker Diamond, who closed and fired from a short distance, shooting 'huge pieces' off his target. The enemy fighter then went into an uncontrollable spin and smashed into the frozen earth below. Seconds later Maj Halton scored

The horrible weather conditions experienced by the 352nd FG at Asch during December 1944 are clearly evidenced by this photo of Lt Littge commencing his take-off run from Asch in 44-11330 (*Ralph Littge*)

Yellow Flight's second kill of the morning, and simultaneously Lt Ray Littge of White Flight added a third to the list. Littge stated in his report;

'I then bounced a '109 shooting at a P-51. This enemy aircraft broke for the deck immediately, and I started shooting from 800 yards down to 150 yards, seeing many strikes and setting the left wing on fire. The fire stopped after a little while, and he climbed to 6000 ft and bailed out.'

Five minutes later Lt Col Meyer's section knocked another 4.5 fighters out of the sky, these kills being credited to 'J C', who downed one and shared a second Bf 109 with a pilot from another group, Capts Ralph Hamilton and Marion Nutter and Lt Alexander Sears, all three of whom downed a Bf 109 apiece.

Later that day the 487th FS was patrolling near Vellendor when someone noticed a formation of about thirty Bf 109s flying on the deck. In an instant the 'Bluenosers' peeled off and hit the unsuspecting German formation with a vengeance. The first two Bf 109s fell away being ripped apart by the gunfire of Lt Col Meyer and Lt James Bateman.

As these fighters crashed, Lts Duerr Schuh and William C Miller moved in and destroyed four more. Schuh despatched two of the Bf 109s within seconds of each other, and then covered Miller's tail as he shot down another Bf 109 from this hapless formation. As Miller's victim crashed, Schuh pulled in behind another Messerschmitt and smashed its right wing with a long burst, then watched it roll over and crash. As this Bf 109 hit the ground, the remaining German pilots in the formation apparently woke up and hastily departed the scene. By then Duerr Schuh had claimed the three aerial victories he needed to 'make ace'.

The 487th FS suffered the group's only casualty on the 27th when Lt Carl Tafel was shot down and killed by enemy fighters near Heimerzheim.

That night the Germans made an attempt at avenging their recent heavy losses by bombing Y-29. The attack was noted by Iggy Marinello (328th FS) in his diary;

'That night the angry Huns came over low and brought everything in the book with them. The field guns went off, the sky was filled with tracers and the foxholes were full of GIs. Eight alerts and not much sleep. Little damage was done, but plenty of action. The next day was spent building more foxholes. War was now a serious thing to us peace-loving fellows. We walked to and from the line carrying our guns, ammo, helmets and gas masks. No one was taking any chances. Yes it was rough in Belgium near the frontlines.'

On 27 December, while the groundcrews continued the improvement of defences around Y-29, the pilots headed to Germany. As the 'Bluenosers' approached Bonn, a large gaggle of enemy aircraft was observed and the 486th and 487th FSs peeled off for the attack. The assault began at 1100 hrs, and within 30 minutes the ground was littered with the wreckage of German fighters. Maj Bill Halton had his best day of the war by downing three Bf 109s himself and sharing a fourth with Lt Anthony Goebel. Halton achieved aerial 'acedom' with this haul, as did his squadronmate Lt Ray Littge with his three Fw 190 kills. The quickness of Littge's destruction of these aircraft is borne out in his encounter report;

'Flying White Three, our Flight of four bounced 8+ FW 190s on the deck. They started a loose Lufbury to the left and my wingman, Lt (Russell) Ross, and I got behind the last boy in the Lufbury. I got strikes

After Maj Preddy was reassigned to the 328th FS, his *CRIPES A' MIGHTY 3RD* was reassigned to Capt Henry Stewart (four aerial kills and one strafing victory), who renamed it *The Margarets* and changed the code to 'HO-N' – see photo on page 110. The fighter was assigned next to Capt Marion Nutter (four aerial kills), who retained the code but renamed it *Sexshunate*. Unfortunately this famous Mustang (which should have been preserved for a museum) was lost to flak on 16 April 1945, and its pilot, Lt Walter Padden (two strafing victories), killed (*352nd FG Association*)

on his wings and tail, and he immediately snapped to the left and hit the ground and exploded. This is verified by Lt Ross's statement. I got behind another one and scored many strikes on the cockpit and wing root area. He rolled over on his back and went into the ground.

'In the meantime all but one of the '190s were either shot down or dispersed, and I started turning with him. I got strikes on him several different times. He straightened out, jettisoned his canopy and started pulling up. Then an unidentified P-51 came down on him from above and got several strikes as the pilot bailed out.

'I claim three (3) FW 190s destroyed.'

Following Lt Littge in scoring were Lt Col John Meyer (487th), Capt Marion Nutter (487th) and Lts Richard Henderson and William Reese (both of the 486th) with two each. Lt Col Willie O Jackson (486th), Maj Franklyn Greene (486th) and Lts James Bateman (487th), Sanford Moats (487th), Earl Lazear (486th), Russell Ross (487th) and James Wood (487th) closed out the scoring with one each. The solitary Bf 109 claimed by Earl Lazear gave him ace status.

By 1130 hrs the enemy formation had been totally routed, and the 'Bluenosers' returned to Y-29 with 22 victories and no losses.

The weather began to deteriorate on 28 December, and although the 352nd continued to fly missions, encounters were non-existent for the next few days. The increasing cold and new snow was making life miserable for the 'Bluenosers', and the search for fuel for their camp stoves became the preoccupation of all personnel during this period. Yet in spite of the horrible conditions the groundcrews somehow kept their Mustangs operational, and numerous sorties were flown on a daily basis.

The missions of 28-30 December were virtually uneventful, except for dodging flak from time to time. On the 31st, however, the 328th FS, led on this occasion by Lt Col John Meyer, encountered two of the Luftwaffe's new Arado Ar 234 jet bombers during a patrol. The engagement took place near the Belgian town of Verviers, and Capt Don Bryan made the first bounce on the twin-engined jets. He scored a number of hits on the Ar 234, but had to break away after being warned of the approach of a second Arado. Lt Col Meyer then attacked the second bomber, and after a long chase, finally shot it down near Bonn.

The 352nd also suffered its final fatality of 1944 on this day when the 328th FG's Flt Off Hugh Howard Jr crashed his Mustang into the Channel when his flight ran into bad weather.

BODENPLATTE TO VE-DAY

During the early morning hours of 1 January 1945 an event which had not been seen in Germany for four years was unfolding. The sky was darkened and the ground shook from the sound of 800 low-flying aircraft as they headed westward on what would prove to be the Luftwaffe's final large-scale offensive mission of the war. This was the beginning of Operation *Bodenplatte*, the last desperate attempt by the Luftwaffe to annihilate the Allied air forces based on the Continent. Their targets were 16 airfields located in the low countries and north-eastern France. The Germans believed the destruction of these bases would end Allied air superiority, and allow their fighters to more effectively defend German cities against bombing raids.

In spite of its high hopes, the dreams of the Luftwaffe were shattered by the events that followed. Through sheer determination, its pilots did indeed do considerable damage to Allied facilities, but at a cost the Luftwaffe could not afford. About 200 Allied aircraft were destroyed, but in turn the Germans lost approximately 300 fighters and 232 pilots, 30 of whom were experienced commanders.

Without a doubt the most decisive battle of the day took place over Asch (Y-29), when the 352nd FG teamed up with the 366th FG to smash the

Jim Bleidner, who served as Lt Col John C Meyer's armourer, poses with his P-51B-10 *Lambie II*. Jim's respect for his boss is illustrated by his comments (included on page 107) about Meyer's anticipation of the 1 January 1945 *Bodenplatte* air offensive (*James Bleidner*)

P-51D-15 44-15041 *Petie 3rd* ('HO-M') was the aeroplane in which Lt Col Meyer scored as many as 11.5 of his aerial victories, and yet it was virtually lost to history until this photograph was discovered during the late 1980s in assistant crew chief Bill Kohlhas' personal photo album. Meyer flew 44-15041 in combat between early November 1944 and 1 January 1945 (*William Kohlhas*)

attack. During the course of the engagement, which is now known to the veterans of the 352nd FG as the 'Legend of Y-29', the 487th FS destroyed 24 German fighters. Many former 'Bluenosers' cite this occasion above all others as the one that exemplifies John Meyer's gift for leadership. His armourer, Jim Bleidner, probably stated it best;

'While it is true that he showed extraordinary heroism in that event and many others, it is also true that his planning ahead and ability to "think like a German" played a very important part. In this case, he was convinced that the Germans would believe that the forward airfields would be vulnerable on New Year's Day because the pilots and groundcrews would have hangovers from the night before. He called his pilots together on New Year's Eve and said no parties until the following night. As it happened, he was correct in his analysis.'

The 'Bluenosers' had not been scheduled for an early morning mission, but because of his 'gut feelings' Meyer pressed the Ninth Air Force for permission to fly an early patrol. To ensure the Mustangs would be ready if the mission was approved, the groundcrews set to work in the bitter cold at 0530 hrs to pre-flight the aircraft, and when the approval arrived at 0800 hrs, the 487th FS was prepared.

Across the airstrip the groundcrews of the Ninth Air Force's 366th FG had performed the same chores on their P-47s. The group was already scheduled for a dawn ground attack mission against German positions in the 'Bulge' area, and eight Thunderbolts of the 391st FS would be the first aircraft in the air from Y-29 at 0842 hrs. These machines, armed with 500-lb bombs and rockets, penetrated the heavy ground mist and headed for the Ardennes battle zone.

A second flight of eight P-47s from the 390th FS duly took off at 0915 hrs, and they were just setting course to their target area when Lt Jack Kennedy saw flak bursts north-east of the field and alerted the rest of his flight. Led by Capt Lowell Smith, the flight turned to investigate. While this was happening, the 487th FS was taxying toward the runway.

Just as the 'Bluenosers' had formed into three four-aeroplane flights on the runway, the P-47 pilots spotted the approaching enemy aircraft and

Three of the 487th's pilots that smashed the Luftwaffe's assault on Asch on 1 January 1945 were (from left to right) Sandy Moats (four kills), Bill Halton (one kill) and Ray Littge (two kills). All three men survived the war as aerial aces, although Ray Littge would later perish in a flying accident whilst at the controls of an F-84D Thunderjet on 20 May 1949 and 'Wild Bill' Halton was killed in action when his F-51D was shot down over Korea by Communist Chinese flak on 21 May 1952 (*352nd FG Association*)

attacked. This key 'block' momentarily disrupted the German fighters (from JG 11) that were streaking toward Y-29, and allowed Lt Col Meyer to lead his pilots into this historic battle.

The Germans were not distracted for long though, and the 487th FS literally had to fight its way into the air. Meyer, leading the first flight down the runway, claimed the first of his two kills of the day while still in his take-off climb. As his first victim half rolled and smashed into the ground, Meyer selected another Fw 190 as his second target, and chased it to an area north-west of Liège. After four separate attacks, John Meyer nailed the fighter for his 24th aerial victory of the war. With an additional 13 strafing kills, Lt Col John C Meyer's total now stood at 37, which made him the highest scoring American pilot in the ETO.

The remainder of White Flight jumped right into the action, and Meyer's wingman, Lt Alex Sears, scored next;

'I was flying White 2 on Col Meyer's wing. We had just taken off when we were bounced by 40 or 50 Me109s and FW 190s. One Me109 came at me head-on and we made several passes at each other, both of us firing. On the third pass I got some strikes on his engine and shot part of the tail section away. He started burning and went down in a lazy spiral and crashed.'

White 3, Lt Ray Littge, shot down the first of his two Fw 190s after one quick burst, but the second proved to be a little more difficult. This Focke-Wulf took numerous hits from Littge's guns but just kept on going, even though it was emitting huge clouds of black smoke. Lt Littge kept following and shooting until he was out of ammunition, yet the Fw 190 still did not fall, so the Mustang ace continued the chase until the German fighter finally pulled up and the pilot bailed out in the vicinity of Paris.

White Flight's Lt Alden Rigby, White 4, joined the action by downing an Fw 190 that was on Lt Littge's tail, then broke sharply to the left and bounced another Focke-Wulf. He described the remainder of his mission;

'I dropped down on his tail and my gunsight went out, so I fired a long burst until I noticed hits on his wing roots. He started pouring black smoke and lost altitude until he crashed into the trees. I immediately returned to the field and noticed a P-47 in a Lufbury with a '109. The P-47 fired a short burst and I noticed a few strikes on the tail section of

An unidentified member of Lt Alden Rigby's groundcrew poses with his P-51D-15 44-15629 *Eleen and Jerry* ('HO-R') soon after *Bodenplatte*. Rigby was a major contributor to the 487th FS's success on 1 January 1945, shooting down two Fw 190s and sharing in the destruction of two Bf 109s. In the autumn of 2000 Rigby became the 352nd FG's final ace, when the shared credits for the two Bf 109s were finally upgraded to full credits by the Victory Credit Board (*352nd FG Association*)

the '109. The enemy aircraft seemed to tighten his turn, and as the P-47 mushed to the outside, I came in from beneath and fired a long burst, noticing hits on his wing. Coolant came out and the enemy aircraft crashed into an open field.

'I started circling the field to make a landing because I was almost out of ammo. I investigated what seemed to be another fight a mile or so to my right. I pulled into the fight with two other P-51s. One P-51 fired at the enemy aircraft and scored hits, and then the '109 broke in my direction and I fired the remainder of my ammo at him, scoring at least one hit in the cockpit. The enemy aircraft dived straight into the ground.

'I claim two FW 190s destroyed and two Me 109s destroyed (one possibly shared with an unidentified P-47 and the other possibly shared with an unidentified P-51).'

For the next 55 years Alden Rigby waited to be declared an ace, but these two half victories clouded the issue, and his official score remained four aircraft destroyed. In the autumn of 2000 the Victory Credit Board re-evaluated the claims and gave Alden Rigby full credit for both of the Bf 109s, and he has now officially joined the ranks of World War 2 aces.

Maj Bill Halton's Yellow Flight followed White Flight into the air, and into instant combat. The flight tracked German fighters through the area while dodging intense 'friendly' ground fire, and managed to destroy nine enemy aircraft before returning to land. Lt Sanford Moats shot down four Fw 190s (to take his final wartime tally to 8.5 aerial kills), Lt Henry Stewart was a close second with three Bf 109s (taking his overall tally to four aerial kills) and Maj Halton and Lt Dean Huston each downed an Fw 190.

Sanford Moats provided a vivid description of the action;

'I was flying Yellow 3 in Maj Halton's flight. As I took off I spotted about 15+ FW 190s at 100 ft coming in from three o'clock on their way to make a pass at the airstrip north of our field. At the same time I noticed approximately 15 Me-109s flying top cover at 3500 ft just below a thin cloud cover. Two '190s broke into my wingman, Lt Huston, and myself, and we entered a Lufbury to the left, under intense, light, friendly(!) flak.

'I closed on the first '190 and looked back to see a '190 closing on the tail of my wingman. I called to break as the '190 started shooting at him. I then fired a short burst at 300 yards and 30 degrees deflection at the '190 ahead of me, observing strikes in the cockpit area and left wing root. He burst into flames and I saw him crash and explode as I continued the turn. The pilot did not get out. Approximately 50 enemy aircraft were in the vicinity, and the entire area was full of friendly flak.

'I chased a '190 that was strafing a marshalling yard as my second target. He broke left and started to climb. I fired a short burst at 200 yards and 20 degrees deflection, observing a concentration of strikes on both wing roots. Both wings folded up over the canopy of the enemy aircraft and he dropped straight in. The pilot did not get out. I continued my left turn and rolled out slightly above and behind another '190, which broke left. I fired a short burst and observed hits on the left side of the fuselage, canopy and left wing root. He burst into flames, the canopy came off, and he crashed. The pilot did not get out.

'I then broke into several '109s and '190s who were coming at me from the rear, heading toward Germany. They split up and I picked one '190 who broke into me. We made several head-on passes and I pulled up and

P-51D-5 44-13321 *The Margarets* ('HO-N') was flown by Capt Henry Stewart of the 487th FS. Maj Preddy's former *Cripes A'Mighty 3rd*, this machine was reassigned to Capt Stewart in September 1944 when the unit's leading ace was posted home on 30 days' leave. Stewart failed to claim any of his four aerial victories (three of these were scored on 1 January 1945) with this machine, which he swapped for P-51D-10 44-14716 in November (*352nd FG Association*)

came down on his tail, firing a two-second burst, observing several strikes from wingtip to wingtip. He levelled off and hit the deck. I closed and fired several bursts from dead astern, observing strikes all over the tail and wing sections.

'As we passed over Maastricht I fired a short burst that exploded his belly tank, and my aircraft was hit by 40 mm ground fire. At this time I had only one gun firing, and the enemy aircraft kept taking violent evasive action on the deck as we crossed the front lines. I fired a short burst at him every time I had a chance and observed many strikes on his tail section. I climbed above the enemy aircraft and made an attack from above and to the right. I fired and observed a few strikes around the right wing root. The enemy aircraft broke left, pulled up slightly and dove into the ground. The pilot did not get out.

'I returned to our airdrome and was fired at by ground batteries. A lone Me-109 came across the field and I made a pass at him. He broke up into me and I fired my remaining few rounds of ammo at him at 90 degrees deflection and 100 yards' range. He hit the deck and I chased him into Germany before returning to our airdrome to give it top cover. Another '109 came by and I followed him through a couple of barrel rolls but could not shoot as I was out of ammo. He went straight up, chopped throttle, tried to get on my tail, couldn't, stalled out, recovered and split-essed at 1500 ft, barely pulling out over the trees. Another P-51 came into the area at this time and shot the enemy aircraft down four miles north-east of the field. I later found out that the pilot of the P-51 was Capt Stewart.

'All enemy aircraft were aggressive, and the last '109 was absolutely hot. We were all handicapped by fuselage fuel tanks and by ground fire, and I feel very proud of our 12-ship squadron destroying 23 bandits on take-off without loss. Claim: 4 FW 190s.'

By the time Capt Bill Whisner's Blue Flight lifted from the runway the sky was filled with low flying enemy aircraft, and Whisner scored his first kill of the day while still climbing. His encounter report stated;

'As I pulled my wheels up after taking off I heard over the radio-transmitter that there were bandits east of the field. We didn't take time to form up, but set course, wide open, straight for the bandits. There were a few P-47s mixing it up with the bandits as I arrived. I ran into about 30 FW-190s at 1500 ft. There were many '109s above them. I picked out a '190 and pressed the trigger. Nothing happened. I reached down and turned on my gun switch and gave a couple of good bursts. As I watched him hit the ground and explode, I felt myself being hit. I broke sharply to the right and up. A '190 was about 50 yards behind me, firing away.

'As I was turning with him, another P-51 attacked him and he broke off his attack on me. I then saw that I had several 20 mm holes in each wing and another round hit my oil tank. My left aileron was also out and I was losing oil, but my temperature and pressure were steady.

'Being over friendly territory, I could see no reason for landing immediately so I turned toward a big dogfight, and shortly had another '190 in my sights. After I hit the '190 with several bursts, its pilot tried to jump. Just as his canopy came off I fired again and the '190 rolled over, crashed and exploded.

'There were several '109s in the vicinity so I engaged one of them. We fought for five or ten minutes and I finally managed to get behind him. I hit him good and he tumbled to the ground. At this time I saw 15-20 fires from crashed aeroplanes. Bandits were reported strafing the field so I headed for the strip.

'I saw a '109 strafe the north-eastern portion of the strip. I started after him and he turned into me. We made two head-on passes and on the second I hit him in the nose and wings. The '109 crashed and burned east of the airstrip. After it crashed I chased several more bandits, but they

Lt Merton 'Smokey' Stover's P-51D-5 44-13871 *"Ellie"* is seen at rest on a blanket of snow at Bodney. This machine was scrapped in late November 1944 after being badly shot up during a mission. Note the standard USAAF blister hangar in the background, which provided shelter for two Mustangs. These quickly-erected structures proved essential when heavy maintenance had to be performed in this sort of weather (*352nd FG Association*)

evaded me in the clouds. By now my windshield was covered with oil, so I headed back to the strip and landed.'

So impressive was this performance that both the squadron and the participating pilots were decorated. The 487th FS was presented with the Distinguished Unit Citation, which was a unique honour since this award was usually reserved for units the size of a group or larger. Individual decorations included DSCs for Lt Col John C Meyer (his third), Capt William T Whisner (his second) and Lt Sanford Moats, and Silver Stars for Lt Col William Y Halton, Capt Henry M Stewart, Lt Raymond Littge and Lt Alden Rigby.

Another very unique aspect to this battle was that the groundcrews finally got to witness their pilots in action. John Meyer was extremely proud of the 487th's performance, and in his tribute to the men of the unit he noted the importance of the groundcrews in an almost poetic fashion;

'This day was particularly important to the crew chiefs of the 352nd FG. In a year and a half of sweat and tears their only knowledge of the war was the stories their pilots told, the missing faces, torn aircraft, and sometime bloody cockpits. Until now these men had lived on the fringe of the crusade in Europe and had nothing to show for their large contribution but a solitary European Theater Ribbon on their jackets. Until now they had even been denied the self-satisfying fruition of the tortured mind and aching hearts behind their skilled hands.

'On January 1, they stood out 100 strong, each man on the edge of his foxhole, never venturing to get in it, in order that he might see the skilful pilot employing the aeroplane which he had inspired with the caressing hands of a lover the night before, destroy the enemy in flaming cauldrons well within the reach of his own eyes. Fifteen of the enemy aircraft came down within a mile of the field.'

Meyer was equally praiseworthy of the efforts of those pilots from the 487th who succeeded in getting airborne on this day;

'For the first time in my experience in the European air war American fighters had neither the advantage of superior tactical position, numbers or equipment. For the first time there was no measurement involved in the final determination other than the relative skill and initiative of the pilots. It was no time for leadership or organisation. It was man against man.'

As it turned out 1 January 1945 would see Lt Col John C Meyer fly his final combat missions of the war. After returning from his second sortie of the day, he was alerted for another assignment, but several days later an accident involving the ammunition carrier he was travelling in and a snow-covered Belgian road left Meyer with a serious leg injury. Shortly thereafter he was sent home for rest and recuperation.

Following the battle over Y-29 things quietened down, and for nearly two weeks the sky was devoid of enemy aircraft. The 'milk runs' finally came to an end on 14 January when over 900 Eighth Air Force

Another rare view of Lt Col Meyer's P-51D-15 44-15041 *Petie 3rd*, the fighter being photographed whilst taxying out for a mission from Chiévres during February 1945. By now the aircraft had been assigned to Lt James N Wood, and he changed the code letters from 'HO-M' to 'HO-Z'. Later the name and all but five of John Meyer's kill markings (Wood claimed three aerial victories and one strafing kill) were removed, Lt Wood renaming the fighter *Ricky* (*352nd FG Association*)

bombers headed toward the oil refineries in central Germany. Waiting for the strike force were huge formations of Luftwaffe aircraft, and on this date the fighter pilots of the Eighth Air Force would set a new record by downing 161 enemy fighters for the loss of only 16 of their own.

The battle was already about two hours old when the 352nd FG joined the action over Holland. The 486th FS encountered and engaged an unusually aggressive flight of 12 Fw 190s, eight Mustangs bouncing the German fighters. Instead of the fight breaking up into individual battles, the Focke-Wulfs stayed together in an ever descending Lufbery circle. This manoeuvre lasted from about 9000 ft down to approximately 5000 ft, when some of the Fw 190s tried to escape. These attempts were made in vain, however, and within minutes six of them had been shot down.

Two of the enemy fighters were gunned out of the sky by Lt William Reese (taking his overall tally of aerial kills to four), and Lts Ernest Bostrom and Earl Mundell each claimed one – Bostrom's kill gave him ace status. The remaining two were shared by Lts George Contos and John Stearns, and Contos and an unidentified pilot from the 4th FG.

After its devastating defeat on 14 January, the German fighter force again went into hiding and was not seen again by the 'Bluenosers' until the 23rd. The 486th FS was once more the centre of activity, for after receiving a vector to the vicinity of the German town of Neuß, Red Flight found two Bf 109s trying to bounce a flight of dive-bombing P-47s. Lt Lumir Vitek peeled off and led his flight after the Messerschmitts, and the enemy aircraft tried to evade by flying through some sparse clouds, but without success. Finally, in a desperate attempt to get away, one of the Bf 109s headed for the deck, but Lt Vitek stayed right with him. The fighter was hit repeatedly by Vitek's gunfire and seriously damaged, before Lt Contos zoomed in and added the finishing touch just as the pilot jumped.

German fighters were up early the following morning, and this time it was the 487th FS that engaged them. The action took place over Wahn airfield, and Lt Ray Littge got things going by downing a Bf 109 in the landing pattern. Moments later Lt Col Bill Halton caught another unsuspecting Messerschmitt and destroyed it with a well placed burst.

Later in the day the 328th FS lost its commanding officer during an engagement in the same sector. The patrol, led by Maj Earl Abbott, had

Maj Earl Abbott, CO of the 328th FS, and his P-51D-10 44-14710 *Flossie III* ('PE-A'). A hugely experienced pilot, Abbott lost his life in this Mustang on 25 January 1945 over Aachen whilst on his 92nd combat mission in the ETO. He had claimed 4.75 aerial victories and one strafing kill, as well as one damaged in the air and three on the ground (*352nd FG Association*)

Lt Bobby Dodd's P-51K-5 44-11626 *"It's SUPERMOUSE"/SWEET SUE* at Bodney in April 1945. The lettering in the fighter's nickname had originally been applied in red, but this was changed to black in late April 1945 (*Robert W Dodd*)

Capt Ed Heller's P-51D-10 44-14696 *HELL-ER BUST* is seen in its 'early' scheme. In this photograph, the pilot's victory markings take the form of black swastikas applied ahead of the left windscreen. Shortly after this shot was taken, the swastikas were removed and replaced by red Iron Crosses under the canopy. Heller's newly-decorated Mustang is illustrated as a colour profile in this volume. One of the 352nd's longest serving pilots, Ed Heller made 'aerial ace' in this machine on 2 March 1945 when he downed an Fw 190. This was his sole aerial victory with the fighter, although he used 44-14696 to claim seven aircraft destroyed on the ground during a series of strafing runs at Ganacker airfield on 16 April 1945 (*352nd FG Association*)

been routine until the unit was vectored towards some enemy aircraft. Lt Robert W Dodd recalled the events that followed;

'We were vectored toward two Me-109s coming from our left about 5000 ft under us. When Maj Abbott saw them he led White Flight down to attack. The '109s saw the diving Mustangs and tried to evade by doing a series of rolls. When Lt Chuck Owens and Maj Abbott tried to roll with them they became separated, and Maj Abbott's Mustang vanished from view. At this point the '109s split up, one heading north and the other heading east.

'While Lt Owens continued after the north-bound '109, the four of us in my flight (Red Flight) followed the east-bound enemy aircraft. All four of us pulled up on the tail of the '109, trying to get a shot at him. (Charles) Goodman and (Elmo) Dubay nailed him. The '109 rolled across a road and through a couple of fences in a ball of fire. What ever happened to Maj Abbott occurred at about this time, and to this day no one knows what happened to him – he just vanished.'

A search for Maj Abbott had to be abandoned shortly after it started because Asch was about to be weathered in. As it turned out this mission was to be the 352nd FG's last from the Belgian airfield, for on 27 January the group's advance party headed toward Chiévres (Y-84), again in Belgium, to prepare the facilities. By early February it was ready.

The first mission flown from Chiévres on 2 February was uneventful, and with the exceptions of some train-busting and one unconfirmed aerial victory by Lt Jim Wood on 6 February, things remained pretty quite until 22 February. A solitary pilot was lost during this period, however, Lt Fred Powell of the 486th FS suffering mechanical failure in his Mustang over the German town of Geldern on the 3rd. He crash-landed near Goch and was captured.

On the 22nd German jets were encountered near Stendal, the 'Bluenosers' taking on four Me 262s. Maj Earl Duncan of the 328th FS was able to damage one of a pair of jets that had just shot down two B-17s, the second jet in turn being forced into the flightpath of the 486th FS. At about the same time, Lt Charles Price of the latter unit saw one of the Me 262s passing right in front of him. His encounter report stated;

'I broke after him and started firing at about 400 yards. My fire hit both of his wings and I saw pieces fall away. I continued firing and then saw several large pieces fall off when one of the jets started smoking. He fell off into a tight spiral going down and I followed through, rolling with him. I continued firing on the way down and saw the whole fuselage burst into flame and explode. Pieces of debris struck my left bomb shackle and I was forced to pull out to prevent a collision with the burning aircraft.'

Lt Bill Gerbe witnessed and confirmed the kill. That was the last aerial engagement of the month.

During the remainder of February the 'Bluenosers' struck targets on the ground, damaging canal barges and rolling stock, but on the 24th the group lost both Lt Joseph Evans of the 328th (PoW) and Lt Fred Jones of the 486th (killed) to flak.

German fighters were up on 2 March when the Eighth Air Force again turned its attention to the petroleum facilities in Germany. Frequent dogfights occurred during the mission, and 66 enemy aircraft were claimed to have been destroyed. The 486th FS contributed six aerial victories (an Fw 189 and five Fw 190s) and then shot up Zwickau airfield, in eastern Germany, damaging several more Focke-Wulf fighters in a strafing attack.

The first dogfight of the day occurred when Capt Ed Heller led a flight of six P-51s into a pack of fifteen Fw 190s and effectively demolished the formation. Five German fighters were destroyed, two probably destroyed

Capt Chet Harker was another 486th FS ETO veteran, serving alongside Ed Heller from 1943 until VE-Day. He flew a series of fighters named *Cile* in honour of his wife, this beautifully decorated P-51D-15 (44-15611) being the last in the line. Resting on a Marston mat hardstand at Chiévres in March 1945, the fighter also features Harker's cloverleaf/horseshoe *LUCK of the IRISH* motif below the cockpit. This machine was later assigned to Lt Glenn Wensch, who renamed it *DIABLO* (*Chester Harker*)

and two damaged. Capt Heller and Lts Eugene Paulson, David Reichman and Charles Price each downed an Fw 190, and the fifth aircraft was shared by Capt Earl Mundell and Lt Lee Kilgo.

Shortly after this engagement Lt Col Willie O Jackson caught an Fw 189 reconnaissance aircraft over an airfield near Prague and promptly shot it down. He and Capt Chet Harker and Lt C C Pattillo then proceeded to damage six aircraft during strafing runs on the field, before heading home.

The massacre of 2 March sent the long suffering Luftwaffe back into hiding, and during the period of 3-13 March, the 352nd FG only encountered one enemy aircraft (a Bf 109 on the 3rd) in the air, and it was shot down near Dresden by Lt William H Sanford of the 328th FS. When the German fighter force did decide to return to the skies on the 14th, Eighth Air Force fighters further reduced its inventory – 17 enemy aircraft fell during the day, four of them jets. One of the latter was credited to 13.333-kill ace Capt Don Bryan, who used his combat experience to the utmost in order to outwit the German pilot.

The Arado Ar 234 had just pulled up from an abortive bomb run on the bridge at Remagen when Bryan noticed a flight of P-47s on the north-west side of the Rhine. He figured that the Arado would turn eastward to avoid them, and anticipating the German pilot's manoeuvre, Bryan turned in a north-easterly direction and waited to spring his trap. The co-operative Ar 234 pilot did the expected, flying right into the path of Bryan's guns.

On his first pass Capt Bryan knocked out the right engine, and then followed the aircraft as it tried some mild evasive turns. With the jet again in his sights, Bryan knocked out the left engine, and the Arado began trailing smoke. The ace completed his encounter report with these remarks;

Lt Jim Wood's personal markings have now replaced those of John Meyer on the latter's P-51D-15 44-15041 *Petie 3rd* (see photo on page 112). Wood renamed the fighter *Ricky* after his nephew, reduced the number of swastikas to reflect his own record (three aerial kills and one strafing victory) and placed his name on the canopy rail. The pilot elected to keep the famous 487th FS emblem below the cockpit (*352nd FG Association*)

The war now over, Lt Duke Lambright enjoys a peaceful flight over England in his P-51K 44-11628 *Geraldine II*. Note that 'buzz' letters ('PE-J') now appear on the undersurface of the left wing so that 'buzz weary' British civilians could easily identify and report the antics of hard flying young pilots with nothing better to do but fly close to the ground! (*352nd FG Association*)

'At about the time I finished firing the Ar 234 rolled over on its back and dived straight into the ground and exploded. Just before hitting the ground the pilot of the enemy aircraft jettisoned his canopy, but he did not get out.'

On 18 March Maj Bill Halton led the 352nd on a freelance fighter sweep to the Berlin area and encountered a mixed flight of Me 262s and Bf 109s. After a brief and indecisive encounter with an Me 262, another Messerschmitt jet fighter and two Bf 109s were spotted near Wriezen on what appeared to be a reconnaissance mission over the Russian front. Maj Halton led the 487th down and attacked the leader of the Bf 109s. The German tried to dive away, but he could not evade Halton's pursuit and was quickly shot down in flames.

Lt Ray Littge followed the second Bf 109 down to the deck, where he and Lt Jim Wood took turns at shooting up the fleeing Messerschmitt and claimed it as a shared kill. The final victory of the day was a reconnaissance Bf 109 shot down by Flt Off James White of the 487th FS.

Several minutes later a number of the 'Bluenosers' began encountering flights of Russian Yak fighters, and in the confusion the 487th's Lt Albert Peterson was shot down by some over-anxious Soviet pilots. Fortunately he survived the incident and was returned to the group on 1 May 1945. Lt Joe Vickery was not so lucky, for the 487th pilot was killed when his Mustang was hit by flak near Schweibus.

Three days later, on 21 March, the 487th lost yet another pilot when Lt Ervin Pryor was killed attempting to crash-land his flak-damaged P-51D at Chiévres.

The 352nd did not get the opportunity to challenge enemy aircraft again until 25 March, and on that date Lt Ray Littge added yet another Me 262 to the scoreboard. The kill took place over Rechlin airfield when Littge caught the jet in its landing approach. After the American's first burst missed, the pilot of the Me 262 realised his predicament and tried some gentle manoeuvres. As he levelled off, Littge fired several long bursts, setting the fighter's right engine on fire. The pilot then jettisoned his canopy, pulled up to 2000 ft and jumped, but his parachute did not open.

The 'Bluenosers' did not escape unscathed on this mission, for the 487th lost its fourth pilot in a week when Lt Wesley Roebuck was almost certainly shot down and killed by one of the Me 262s seen roaming in the Ulzen area.

Action against the German jets resumed on 30 March during an escort mission to Bremen. Just after the bombers had released their ordnance, Lt James Hurley of the 328th FS spied an Me 262 trying to slip in on a straggling B-17. After a 20-minute chase, Hurley was just about ready to give up when he noticed that the jet's engines seemed to have quit smoking.

As the Me 262 began a slight diving turn to the left, Hurley turned inside it. The jet rolled out of its turn at 6000 ft and became an easy target, Hurley firing a long range fusilade with no result, before closing to 150 ft and hitting the jet with a fatal burst. The Me 262 tried to climb and then nosed over and went straight down, exploding on impact. Unfortunately, Lt Hurley's victory over the jet was marred by the loss of Lt Frank McCarthy (328th FS), who crashed to his death near Oldenburg following engine failure during the trip back to base.

As April began, rumours were rampant around Chiévres that the 352nd was moving back to Bodney. This was a definite morale boost for the 'Bluenosers', who were anxious to return to England. However, for the time being the war would be carried on from its Belgian base.

During the first few days of the month the Eighth Air Force experienced a dramatic increase in the number of encounters with German jets, and the bombers began to suffer. The Me 262 bases were heavily bombed on 8-9 April, but the Luftwaffe still managed to get 50+ jets into the air on the 10th.

Even after their massed formation was broken up by the 1st Air Division's escort fighters, the Me 262s still managed to down five B-17s near Oranienburg. Moments later they destroyed five more bombers from the 3rd Air Division. The jets had won the opening round of the day, but as they were to find out, the fight was far from over.

The dramatic turn of events began as the jets began running low on fuel and headed for their bases. When they arrived at their respective airfields, the Me 262 pilots flew into an ambush. Battles broke out all over the sky, and when they were over, 20 of Germany's vaunted jets had gone down under the guns of Eighth Air Force pilots. Three of the kills were claimed by 'Bluenosers', the first falling to the combined gunfire of Lt Col Earl Duncan of the 328th and Maj Richard McAuliffe of the 487th.

A few miles away Lt C A Pattillo of the 487th FS bounced another Me 262 near Ulzen and shot it down after a ten-minute chase. After his victim had crashed, Pattillo continued circling the airfield and managed to damage a second Me 262 before it fled the scene. The final kill of the day came 15 minutes later when Lts Joseph Pritchard and Carlo Ricci of the 487th FS teamed up to shoot down an Me 262 near Neuruppin.

The rumours about the return to Bodney proved to be true, for the movement order came down on 5 April and the advance party was flown out on B-24s that very day. The move took one week to complete, and the 'Bluenosers'' last mission from Chiévres was flown on 12 April 1945.

When the 352nd FG resumed operations from Bodney on 16 April, it did so in a big way. After escorting bombers of the 1st Air Division through the target area, half of the group's Mustangs broke off escort and began looking for airfields. When they flew over the base at Gonecker approximately 70 aircraft were observed around its perimeter, and Lt Col Willie O Jackson signalled the attack. His first order of business was to neutralise the flak, as he described in his encounter report;

The Pattillo twins pose with Lt Charles C Pattillo's P-51D-5 44-13737 *Little Rebel* ('PZ-W'). Lt Cuthbert A Pattillo is on the right and Charles is on the left. Both had joined the 352nd FG in December 1944, Charles being assigned to the 486th FS and Cuthbert to the 487th. Cuthbert was shot down by flak whilst attacking Ganacker airfield on 16 April 1945, having destroyed two aircraft on the ground just moments earlier. Participating in his 36th mission, Pattillo bailed out of his P-51K-5 44-11556 *Sweet & Lovely* ('HO-Y') and was captured. His brother was credited with five ground kills at Ganacker, thus making him a strafing ace. The Pattillo brothers both remained in the air force post-war, and eventually retired as generals after long and very successful careers (*Sheldon Berlow*)

'We decided to hit the airfield with one section drawing flak, another busting flak and the third as top cover. I took my flight across first from south-west to north-east, not firing, and 15-20 guns opened up. After four or five passes most of those were neutralised by the flak-busters, and a gunnery pattern was set up'.

During the next 30 minutes the 'Bluenosed' Mustangs hammered the field, leaving it a burning wreck. The pilots claimed a total of 40 aircraft destroyed and 27 damaged following the attack, Lt Col Jackson personally accounting for four destroyed and three damaged. Capt Ed Heller set the pace by destroying seven aircraft, and he was closely followed by Lt Cuthbert Pattillo who destroyed six and damaged one. Seven other aircraft were destroyed by pilots of the 486th FS, bringing the squadron's tally for the day to 24.

Capt Ray Littge of the 487th FS also had a good day, destroying three aircraft and damaging five others. His squadronmates added another seven destroyed and eight damaged to the score, but two pilots from this unit were lost in the action. Lt Walter Padden died after his Mustang was downed by flak, and Lt Charles Pattillo was shot down but evaded capture. The remainder of the day's tally went to the 328th FS, which destroyed seven and damaged eight.

16 April had been an incredible day for the Eighth Air Force, for its fighter pilots had destroyed no fewer than 752 aircraft for the loss of 34. The destruction of the Luftwaffe continued the following day when Eighth Air Force fighters chalked up a further 286 aircraft destroyed and 113 damaged. The 352nd FG's contribution to this total was 66 aircraft destroyed and 24 damaged, and Capt Ray Littge set the pace with six kills. The large totals of aircraft destroyed and damaged on these missions

might imply easy scoring, but Capt Littge's account of Red Flight's activities on 17 April show otherwise;

'After leaving the bombers we came upon Prattling airfield, with 75+ single- and twin-engined aircraft parked in dispersals and around the field. Red flight made several passes at flak positions first, effectively silencing them. During these attacks my oil tank was hit and I lost most of my oil, one of my guns was shot out and two electrical lines and the manifold pressure line were also hit. We then went in to strafe. I made seven passes.

'My first two passes were at an Me 262 on the north-eastern corner of the field, which blew up after my second pass. I then attacked and set fire to an Me-109 on the north side. On each of my next three passes I set afire Me-109s in revetments on the south side of the field, and on my last pass I blew up another Me 262 on the north-east corner of the field.

'F/O Frum claims three FW-190s destroyed and two damaged. I saw two of his aeroplanes on fire. Lt Reed claims four Me-109s destroyed and one damaged.

'Lt Myron Reynolds was MIA (he was killed) on this mission. He made at least four or five passes, and I saw a '190 on fire after he attacked it. Lt Reed also saw this ship on fire, as well as an Me-109. When I left the airfield there were at least 70+ fires and burned out fires.'

Three other pilots qualified as strafing 'aces in a day' on this mission. Lts James White and Karl Waldron of the 487th FS and Lt Joseph Carter of the 486th FS each destroyed five enemy aircraft during their passes over the airfield. Col Jim Mayden and Lt Carl Weber of the 328th nearly shared the honour when they destroyed four aircraft apiece.

This mission turned out to be the 'last hurrah' for the 352nd FG. During its remaining five missions before VE-Day no enemy aircraft were encountered, and the flights passed uneventfully except for the loss of Lt John Reiners of the 328th FS, who died on 19 April when his Mustang crashed whilst taking off. The 352nd flew its final mission on 3 May.

Between 9 September 1943 and 3 May 1945 the 352nd FG flew 420 combat missions and destroyed 792.5 aircraft, 505.5 of which were shot down in aerial combat. Twenty-eight pilots qualified as aces in aerial combat, and when using the war-time Eighth Air Force scoring system, which gave full credit for strafing kills, the group's ace list almost doubles to 52.

During its long campaign, the 352nd FG lost 70 pilots and 118 aircraft (plus Lt Glen St John of the 328th FS, who was killed in a flying accident on 7 July 1945). Its pilots received the collective total of 13 DSCs, 31 Silver Star Medals, 336 DFCs, 1304 Air Medals and 42 Bronze Star Medals (these figures include Oak Leaf Clusters, which signify an additional award of the medal to an individual).

No unit history would be complete without acknowledging the hard work of the groundcrews. Without their dedication and skill, the 352nd FG could not have achieved its extraordinary combat record. The closeness of the pilots and their crews has endured through the years, and at the final reunion of the 352nd FG Association in September 2000, a portion of the ceremony was dedicated to these devoted men.

At war's end the 352nd FG was inactivated, and in 1946 the group was re-designated as the 113th FG (later 113th Tactical Fighter Wing) and assigned to the Washington DC Air National Guard. The 328th FS was in turn allocated to the Virginia Air National Guard.

APPENDICES

APPENDIX 1

352nd FG ACES

Rank/Name	Air	Ground	TOTAL	Unit(s)
Lt Col John C Meyer	24	13	37	487th, HQ 352nd
Maj George E Preddy	26.833	5	31.833	487th/328th
Capt Raymond H Littge	10.5	13	23.5	487th
Capt Edwin L Heller	5.5	16.5	22	486th
Capt John F Thornell Jr	17.5	2	19.5	328th
Capt William T Whisner	15.5	3	18.5	487th
Lt Glennon T Moran	13	3	16	487th
Maj Steven W Andrew	9	6.5	15.5	486th
Lt Carl J Luksic	8.5	7	15.5	487th
Capt Woodrow Anderson	4.5	9	13.5	486th
Capt Henry J Miklajcyk	7.5	6	13.5	486th
Capt Donald S Bryan	13.333	0	13.333	328th
Capt Clarence O Johnson	7	6	13	487th/479th FG
Lt Col William T Halton	10.5	2	12.5	328th/487th
Lt Col Willie O Jackson	7	4	11	486th
Capt Frank A Cutler	7.5	3	10.5	486th
Lt Karl M Waldron Jr	3	7	10	487th
Lt Col Everett M Stewart	7.833	1.5	9.333	328th/355th FG/4th FG
Capt Clayton E Davis	5	4	9	487th
Capt Virgil K Meroney	9	0	9	487th
Capt Charles J Cesky	8.5	0	8.5	328th
Capt Sanford K Moats	8.5	0	8.5	487th
Lt Malcolm C Pickering	4	4	8	487th
Maj Walter E Starck	7	0	7	487th
Lt Carl Weber	0	7	7	328th
Capt John D Coleman	4.333	2.5	6.833	328th
Lt William E Furr	3.5	3	6.5	328th
Lt Charles E Goodman	4.5	2	6.5	328th
Capt Francis W Horne	5.5	1	6.5	328th
Lt Alden P Rigby	5	1	6	487th
Capt Alexander F Sears	5	1	6	487th
Col James D Mayden	2	4	6	HQ 352nd
Lt Charles C Pattillo	0	6	6	486th
Capt Alton J Wallace	3	3	6	486th
Lt Donald Y Whinnem	1	5	6	486th
Maj Earl L Abbott	4.75	1	5.75	328th
Lt Charles J Bennette	2	3.5	5.5	328th
Lt Robert H Berkshire	4.5	1	5.5	487th
Lt Joseph D Carter	0.5	5	5.5	486th
Maj Donald H Higgins	2.5	3	5.5	486th

Rank/Name	Air	Ground	TOTAL	Unit
Lt Richard C Brookins	4.25	1	5.25	328th
Lt Edmund Zellner	3.25	2	5.25	328th
Capt Ernest O Bostrom	5	0	5	486th
Capt Ralph Hamilton	4	1	5	487th
Capt Earl R Lazear Jr	5	0	5	486th
Capt Robert G MacKean	0	5	5	486th
Col Joseph L Mason	5	0	5	HQ 352nd
Lt Raymond D Phillips	2	3	5	328th
Capt Duerr H Schuh	5	0	5	487th
Capt William J Stangel	5	0	5	328th
Capt Henry M Stewart	4	1	5	487th
Lt Henry S Sykes	0	5	5	487th

APPENDIX 2

352nd FG BASES

Mitchel Field, New York (328th FS)	1/10/42
Bradley Field, Connecticut	1/10/42
Westover Field, Massachusetts	1/11/42
Trumbull Field, Connecticut	15/1/43
Mitchel Field, New York (328th FS)	17/2/43
Farmingdale, New York (21st PS)	8/3/43
Mitchel Field, New York (34th PS)	8/3/43
Westover Field, Massachusetts	24/5/43
Camp Kilmer, New Jersey	16/6/43
Queen Elizabeth (New York embarkation)	1/7/43
Arrived in Clyde, Scotland	5/7/43
Temporary Stay – Watton airfield, England	8/7/43
AAF Station 141, Bodney, England (approx)	15/7/43
AAF Station Y-29, Asch, Belgium	23/12/44
AAF Station Y-84, Chiévres, Belgium	27/1/45
AAF Station 141, Bodney, England	13/4/45
Queen Mary (homeward bound)	4/11/45
Camp Kilmer, New Jersey, and deactivation	10/11/45

APPENDIX 2

352nd FG GROUP COMMANDERS

Lt Col Edwin M Ramage	30/9/42 to 18/5/43
Col Joe L Mason	18/5/43 to 24/7/44
Col James D Mayden	24/7/44 to 9/45
Lt Col William T Halton	9/45 to 11/45

Squadron Commanders

328th FS

Capt John H Poston	1/10/42 to 7/4/43
Maj Everett W Stewart	7/4/43 to 27/1/44
Maj Harold G Lund	27/1/44 to 11/3/44
Maj I B 'Jack' Donalson	11/3/44 to 21/3/44
Maj Willie O Jackson	21/3/44 to 19/4/44
Maj Harold G Lund	19/4/44 to 21/7/44
Lt Col John C Edwards	21/7/44 to 27/10/44
Maj George E Preddy	27/10/44 to 26/12/44
Maj Earl L Abbott	26/12/44 to 31/1/45
Capt Donald S Bryan	31/1/45 to 4/45
Lt Col Earl D Duncan	4/45 to 9/45

486th FS

Capt William J Hennon	1/10/42 to 1/4/43
Maj Luther H Richmond	1/4/43 to 19/4/44
Maj Willie O Jackson	19/4/44 to 21/2/45
Lt Col Franklyn N Greene	21/2/45 to 26/5/45
Maj Donald H Higgins	26/5/45 to 9/45

487th FS

Maj John C Meyer	1/10/42 to 21/11/44
Maj William T Halton	21/11/44 to 9/45

COLOUR PLATES

1

P-47C-1 41-6135 of the 487th FS at Mitchel Field, New York, Spring 1943

This P-47C, and its stablemates, was used throughout the group's training period on the east coast of the USA. The 352nd experienced some serious mechanical problems with these early-build Thunderbolts during training, suffering a number of fatalities as a result.

2

P-47D-2 42-8007/*HELEN OF TROY* of Lt Clarence J Palmer, 487th FS, Bodney, September 1943

Palmer completed 85 missions (301 combat hours) between September 1943 and August 1944, flying two assigned P-47Ds (this particular aircraft was the first one) followed by two P-51Bs, all of which were named *Helen of Troy*. This particular aircraft suffered a collapsed starboard undercarriage leg after experiencing a rough landing at Bodney in early October 1943. Palmer was issued with P-47D-2 42-8382 as a replacement, which he proceeded to fly until the 487th FS converted to P-51Bs in the spring of 1944. He was credited with a strafing kill in 42-8382 and two aerial kills with P-51B-15 42-106901 (his second P-51).

3

P-47D-5 42-8491/*Donna Dae III* of Lt Leo Northrup, 486th FS, Bodney, November 1943

Lt Leo Northrup crash-landed P-47D-5 42-8491 *Donna Dae III* near Bodney at the end of a bomber escort mission to Germany on 5 November 1943. He subsequently flew both a P-51B and a P-51D christened *Donna Dae* (named in honour of his favourite Hollywood actress) during his ETO tour, which ended in August 1944. Northrup scored two aerial kills (Bf 109Gs) with the 352nd, on 21 June 1944, east of Warsaw during the Eighth Air Force's first 'Shuttle Mission' to Russia.

4

P-47D-5 42-8447/*"QUEEN CITY MAMA"* of Capt Donald K Dilling, 487th FS, Bodney, December 1943

Dilling was from Cincinnati (known as the 'The Queen City'), in Ohio, and his Thunderbolt was named both for his hometown and for his wife Marcine. Capt Dilling scored all three of his victories in this aircraft, which he was forced to crash-land in France when he became lost in fog and ran out of fuel on 30 December 1943. The thermite grenade that the pilot placed in the cockpit failed to explode, and the Luftwaffe salvaged 42-8447 and later flew it in German markings. Dilling evaded capture, and after a dangerous trip through France and into Spain, he eventually made it back to Bodney.

5

P-47D-5 42-8460/*The Flying Scot!* of Lt Murdock 'Scottie' Cunningham, 486th FS, Bodney, January 1944

42-8460 was the first of two aircraft to carry this name, the fighter also displaying artwork of a locomotive pulling a long train. Lt Cunningham was credited with one aerial victory and 1.5 strafing kills during his tour, which lasted from September 1943 through to June 1944. All of these successes were scored in P-51B-10 42-106472.

6

P-47D-5 42-8412/*"Sweetie"* of Lt Col Luther Richmond, CO of the 486th FS, Bodney, January 1944

Most USAAF squadrons had an unofficial artist whose job it was to adorn aircraft with (predominantly 'girlie') nose art. The 486th FS had Nilan Jones, and a fine example of his Vargas-inspired handiwork is seen here on squadron CO Maj Luther Richmond's P-47D-5 42-8412. Richmond flew the bulk of his 67 combat missions in this machine.

7

P-47D-2 42-8381/*Little One* of Capt Donald S Bryan, 328th FS, Bodney, February 1944

The 328th FS's Capt Donald S Bryan flew P-47D-2 42-8381 *Little One* (which he named for his wife Frances) in combat from September 1943 through to April 1944, when he received P-51B-5 43-6894. The fighter's mission board shows 53 combat sorties completed, and four kill symbols are proudly worn beneath the cockpit. Bryan, who would finish his tour with the 352nd FG as CO of the 328th FS (having scored 13.333 aerial kills), claimed his first 3.833 victories with 42-8381. Once the 328th FS converted to P-51s in late April 1944, *Little One* soldiered on as 'LJ-P' with the 3rd Gunnery & Tow-Target Flight, based at East Wretham, in Norfolk.

8

P-47D-5 42-26320/*Pattie II* of Lt Lawrence 'Mac' McCarthy, 328th FS, Bodney, February 1944

This was the second of four fighters that Lt McCarthy named after his wife Pattie. 42-26320 was also his most successful mount, for he claimed two Bf 110s destroyed and two damaged with it on 20 February 1944. McCarthy's remaining shared aerial kill was claimed in P-51B-5 43-6906 on 12 June. He completed two tours with the 328th.

9

P-47D-5 42-8439/*Slender, Tender and Tall* of Capt William T Halton, 328th FS, Bodney, February 1944

This was the first of three fighters flown by Halton that were named *Slender, Tender and Tall*, but it was the only one to feature 'Bugs Bunny' artwork – see profile 49 for Halton's last ETO machine. The future 10.5-kill ace scored his first victory (a Bf 109) in 42-8439 on 20 February 1944.

10

P-47D-5 42-8473/*Sweet LOUISE*/*Mrs Josephine*/*Hedy* of Capt Virgil K Meroney, 487th FS, Bodney, March 1944

The only P-47 assigned to the 352nd's lone Thunderbolt ace, 42-8473 was used by Virgil Meroney to claim all nine of his aerial kills, scored between 1 December 1943 and 16 March 1944. The trio of female names that adorned the fighter were inspired by the wives of the crew – *Sweet LOUISE* was Capt Meroney's wife, *Josephine* was the wife of crew chief S/Sgt Albert Giesting and *Hedy* was the wife of assistant crew chief Sgt Jack Gillenwater. Al Giesting relates that Capt Meroney was so possessive about this aeroplane that if he went on leave, the P-47 went into maintenance so no one else could fly it! However, this ploy did not prevent squadronmate, and future ranking ace of the 352nd FG, Capt George Preddy from claiming his second victory (an 'Me 210') in 42-8473 east of the Zuider Zee on 22 December 1943.

11

P-51B-15 42-106832/*WE THREE* of Lt Edmond Zellner, 328th FS, Bodney, May 1944

Lt Zellner scored all of his 3.25 aerial and two strafing kills in this Mustang. On 19 May 1944 he shared in the destruction of a Bf 109 and claimed a second Messerschmitt as a probable. Zellner's next kills came 48 hours later when he destroyed two elderly Ju 86 bombers on the ground at Altruppin airfield, in Germany. On 24 May he downed a Bf 109, and three days later Zellner followed this up with another Messerschmitt fighter shot down, and a shared kill over an Fw 190. Ed Zellner was subsequently brought down by flak on his 90th mission, his P-51D being hit by flak near Charleroi on 31 July. Bailing out south-west of Brussels, he evaded capture and eventually returned to the UK.

12

P-51B-5 43-6685/*Umbriago* of Lt Robert Frascotti, 486th FS, Bodney, May 1944

This OD Malcolm-hooded P-51B was flown by the popular Lt Robert Frascotti, who had joined the 486th FS in September 1943 and had completed 88 missions up to 6 June 1944. Frascotti became the 352nd's only fatality on D-Day (two other pilots were lost to flak and made PoWs) when *Umbriago* collided with the unfinished new control tower at Bodney as he took off in the dark, early morning hours of 6 June. This was scheduled to be Frascotti's final mission before returning to the USA.

13

P-51B-5 43-6704/*HELL-ER-BUST* of Lt Edwin Heller, 486th FS, Bodney, May 1944

This Mustang was one of the first of its type assigned to the 486th FS. Its pilot, Lt Ed Heller, was one of the tallest aviators in the Eighth Air Force, and he struggled to fit his rangy frame beneath the B-model's original 'birdcage' canopy. Therefore, once clear vision Malcolm hoods became available in the early spring of 1944, his Mustang was immediately allocated a new canopy. Heller scored three aerial and several strafing victories in this machine to open his account in the ETO. He also used the fighter during the Russian 'Shuttle Mission' in late June, during which *HELL-ER-BUST* suffered battle damage en route to the USSR, followed by accidental damage during two aborted departures from Piryatin. He had an engine quit on his first take-off attempt, which resulted in a bent propeller blade when the fighter ran into a ditch. The damage took several days to repair, and 43-6704 then suffered a massive engine failure when Heller once again tried to depart. He eventually left Russia a fortnight after the rest of the group, and 'then spent the next two weeks in Tehran on the john because of a case of dysentery'! The Mustang had suffered hydraulic failure upon departure from Piryatin, and this had to be fixed in Persia. Once both he and his fighter were declared fit, Heller continued his solo trip home via Cairo, Benghazi and Casablanca, where, Heller related, 'a resident general had his eyes on my Mustang and I was summarily grounded'. *HELL-ER-BUST* remained in Casablanca, and its pilot returned to Bodney in a transport aircraft.

14

P-51B-10 42-106661/*Hot Stuff* of Maj Willie O Jackson Jr, CO of the 486th FS, Bodney, May 1944

'Willie O' Jackson's P-51B-10 displayed a beautifully painted 'Vargas girl', appropriately named *Hot Stuff* (note the sizzling effect on the letters) below the cockpit. The fighter's solitary victory symbol denotes Jackson's first confirmed aerial kill, which he scored flying his assigned P-47D-5 42-8452 on 20 February 1944. The seven-kill ace failed to make even a damaged claim in *Hot Stuff* before 'she' was shot down by flak near Le Merterault, in France, on 7 June 1944. The Mustang's pilot on this occasion was Maj Ed Gignac, who died in the crash.

15

P-51B-5 43-7022/*Little Rebel* of Lt Alton J 'Al' Wallace, 486th FS, Bodney, May 1944

This Mustang was one of the first seven P-51Bs received by the 352nd FG, arriving at Bodney on 1 March 1944. Assigned to Lt Al Wallace, the fighter participated in the 486th FS's history-making mission on the 8th of that month when the group put up a split force of Mustangs and Thunderbolts. More significantly, this fighter was used by Capt Ed Gignac to down a Bf 109 during the course of the mission, thus registering the 352nd's first Mustang victory. On 15 April 1944 Lt Wallace scored his first two aerial kills in *Little Rebel*, and he finished the month off with three strafing victories again in 43-7022.

16

P-51B-10 42-106483/*Miss Lace* of Lt Donald McKibben, 486th FS, Bodney, May 1944

This aircraft also featured artwork of the 'Dragon Lady' from the wartime comic strip *Terry and the Pirates* on its port side. The latter was applied in this position simply because it was more visible when McKibben parked his machine in its allotted place on the 486th flightline! He shot down a Bf 109 on 19 April 1944 while flying this aircraft, but less than a month later, on 13 May, *Miss Lace* was destroyed when Capt Frank Cutler collided with a Bf 109 during an air battle over Germany. Cutler was killed.

17

P-51B-10 42-106502/*Opal LEE* of Lt Fred M Allison, 487th FS, Bodney, May 1944

The aircraft was named for Lt Allison's wife, and he scored two strafing victories in it on 11 and 28 April, followed by 1.5 aerial kills on 12 May.

18

P-51B-10 42-106471/*Lambie II* of Lt Col John C Meyer, CO of the 487th FS, Bodney, May 1944

The application of 42-106471's nickname (the origin of which has remained a mystery throughout the years) went through various stages. Initially it appeared in black script, but when the 352nd's famous swept back blue nose marking was added to the Mustang in then spring of 1944, the colour was first changed to yellow and then to the shades illustrated in this profile. Meyer truly came into his own as a fighter ace in this P-51, destroying 5.5 aircraft in the air and six on the ground between 10 April and 12 May 1944. *Lambie II* was destroyed on 7 June 1944 when Lt Clifford Garney spun in near Bodney and was killed while returning from a mission to France.

19

P-51B-10 42-106449/*Princess ELIZABETH* of Lt William T Whisner, 487th FS, Bodney, May 1944

Although Bill Whisner loved Mustangs, he was not happy when the name *Princess ELIZABETH* was applied to his 'HO-W. In a letter to the author, dated 9 February 1988, Whisner related, 'As a boy lieutenant I was coerced into giving the name to the bird by an eager young PIO (Public Information Officer) from New York. Yes it was "the" Elizabeth (Queen Elizabeth) to whom you refer – and it was thought that the favourable publicity would accrue to the group should I do some good things in combat in the '51. However, I immediately succumbed to the kidding and changed the name to what I considered the complete social antithesis – *Moonbeam McSwine*''. The name change occurred when he received his P-51D. Whisner scored one aerial victory in this P-51B, which was lost to flak over France on 6 June 1944. Its pilot, Lt Robert Butler, came down behind Allied lines and was returned to Bodney.

20

P-51B-5 43-7094/*GRACIE*/*Josephine* of Lt Malcolm Pickering, 487th FS, Bodney, May 1944

This aeroplane was named for Lt Pickering's wife Gracie and crew chief S/Sgt Al Giesting's wife Josephine. Pickering scored two of his eight kills in 43-7094, which was eventually shot down by Fw 190s from 5./JG 26 on 23 September 1944, and its pilot, Lt Phanor Waters, killed.

21

P-51B-15 42-106914/*The West "by Gawd" Virginian* of Lt Robert H 'Punchy' Powell Jr, 328th FS, Bodney, June 1944

Powell, a native of West Virginia, named all his aircraft for his home state, and the colours used in the map of West Virginia represent the school colours of his college. While flying this aircraft Powell damaged an Me 410 and a Bf 109 in aerial combat. 42-106914 was destroyed on 18 July 1944 when its engine failed on take-off and Powell crash-landed. Somehow he managed to free himself from the flaming wreckage and escape unharmed.

22

P-51C-10 42-103789/*STRAW BOSS* of Lt Col James D Mayden, HQ 352nd FG, Bodney, Summer 1944

This was the first of two Mustangs Mayden called *STRAW BOSS* during his tour of duty with the 352nd FG, this particular machine being damaged in a wheels up landing at Bodney during the late summer of 1944. Col Mayden is credited with two aerial and four strafing victories.

23

P-51B-10 42-106472/*The FLYING SCOT!!*/*Vicious Virgie* of Lt Carlton Fuhrman, 486th FS, Bodney, June 1944

Lt Fuhrman 'inherited' this aircraft from Lt Murdock 'Scottie' Cunningham and flew it on the first Russian 'Shuttle Mission'. 42-106472 was written off on 12 September 1944 when Lt Glenn Wensch was involved in a landing accident.

24

P-51C-5 42-103758/*The FOX* of Lt James N Wood, 487th FS, Bodney, June 1944

Lt Wood named this machine after high school friend Helen Fox. He flew 45 missions and destroyed 1.5 enemy aircraft in this Mustang, which was still gracing the airfield at Bodney on VE-Day.

25

P-51B-15 43-24807/*STARCK MAD!*/*Even Stevens* of Capt Walter 'Wally' Starck, 487th FS, Bodney, June 1944

The names applied to this Mustang were plays on the surnames of its pilot, Wally Starck, and crew chief, S/Sgt Keith Stevens. Capt Starck claimed two of his seven aerial kills in this P-51B, on 1 and 21 July 1944 (both Bf 109s).

26

P-51B-15 42-106844/*Flossie II* of Maj Earl Abbott, 328th FS, Bodney, July 1944

Named for his wife Florence, Abbott also had a 'Vargas girl' artwork applied to his fighter. He scored two of his 4.75 aerial victories in this Mustang.

27

P-51B-15 42-106872/*PATTY ANN II* of Lt John F Thornell, 328th FS, Bodney, July 1944

Thornell scored nine of his 17.5 aerial victories in *PATTY ANN II*, these being claimed between 8 May and 21 June. Many historians have described this P-51 as being fitted with a Malcolm hood during its operational life, but in reality the replacement hood was actually a Spitfire canopy. *PATTY ANN II* was downed by German fighters on 12 September 1944, killing the pilot, Lt Joseph Broadwater.

28

P-51D-10 44-14151/*PETIE 2ND* of Lt Col John C Meyer, CO of the 487th FS, Bodney, August 1944

The newly married Lt Col Meyer received this aircraft when he returned from leave in the United States, and he christened it *PETIE 2ND*. This profile illustrates how the fighter looked in early August 1944. Over the coming months the colours used to mark its name and kill symbols were changed to orange to make them more noticeable. Meyer only scored two ground kills in this, his best known Mustang. *PETIE 2ND* was quickly, and secretly, replaced by *PETIE 3RD* during the night after young corporal Bernie Howard backed his jeep into the stabiliser and damaged it. Sympathetic crew chief, S/Sgt Bill Conkey, sent *PETIE 2ND* to the maintenance shop and replaced her with *PETIE 3RD* (see profile 38). Legend has it that Lt Col Meyer never knew the story, and after repairs this old fighter became Sheldon Heyer's *Sweetie FACE*, coded 'HO-N'.

29

P-51D-5 44-13878 of Capt John 'Muscles' Bennett, 487th FS, Bodney, August 1944

One of the group's longest serving pilots, Capt Bennett was the only 'Bluenoser' to decorate his Mustangs with a sharksmouth, and all of his assigned P-51s carried this artwork. He flew two tours of duty with the 487th FS, and is credited with a total of three aircraft destroyed in the air and four damaged, as well as one strafing kill. None were scored in this aircraft, however.

30

P-51D-10 44-14397/*EX-LAX...Shht"n"Git!* of Flt Off Cyril B Doleac, 487th FS, Bodney, August 1944

Doleac named this aircraft after a well-known laxative. Someone sent the EX-LAX Corporation a photo of the machine and the framed print duly hung proudly in the corporate headquarters during the war. Doleac is credited with one aerial victory.

31

P-51C-1 42-103320/*Little Ann* of Lt Glennon Moran, 487th FS, Bodney, September 1944

Lt Moran was one of the 487th FS's most aggressive fighter pilots, as his tally clearly illustrates. He was credited with scoring 11 of his 13 aerial victories while flying this Mustang. After Moran completed his tour of duty in August 1944, *Little Ann* (painted on the right side of the fighter's nose) was assigned to Lt Raymond Littge, who renamed her *Silver Dollar*. Littge flew 42-103320 until it was declared war-weary on 29 October 1944, having by then claimed four ground kills with the veteran fighter.

32

P-51D-5 44-13406/*Barbara M. 4TH* of Lt Col John 'Curly' Edwards, CO of the 328th FS, Bodney, September 1944

Edwards was credited with two aerial victories, one of which was claimed in this aircraft (amongst the first D-model Mustangs issued to the 352nd FG) on 13 July 1944.

33

P-51D-10 44-14061/*Little One III* of Capt Donald S Bryan, 328th FS, Bodney, November 1944

Lt Bryan received this P-51D when he returned for his second tour with the 328th FS in the autumn of 1944, and he scored eight of his 13.333 aerial victories with it – five of these were claimed on 2 November 1944. 44-14061 was destroyed during the attack on Asch on 1 January 1945.

34

P-51D-15 44-14877/*PENNIE'S EARL* of Lt Earl Lazear, 486th FS, Bodney, November 1944

Five-kill ace Lt Lazear scored his final two victories in this aircraft on 30 November and 27 December (both Bf 109s). His most successful mission occurred on 12 September 1944 when he downed three Bf 109s near Kyritz, Germany.

35

P-51D-5 44-11330/*E Pluribus Unum* of Lt Raymond Littge, 487th FS, Bodney, November 1944

Lt Littge was assigned this aircraft in October 1944, and he flew it until February 1945. In that time he shot down two Bf 109s on 27 November for his first aerial kills, and then claimed six victories between 26 December and 1 January – it is believed that Littge was flying this aircraft on all of these missions. When 44-11330 was damaged in a landing accident, Littge named its replacement *Miss Helen*.

36

P-51D-5 44-13401/*Diann Ruth II* of Capt Charles Cesky, 328th FS, Asch (Y-29), Belgium, December 1944

8.5-kill ace Capt Cesky downed his final three victories (all Fw 190s) on 25 December 1944 in this P-51D. All bar one of his remaining kills were scored in P-51D-5 44-13927 *Diann*.

37

P-51D-15 44-14906/*Cripes A'Mighty* of Maj George E Preddy, CO of the 328th FS, Asch (Y-29), Belgium, December 1944

Maj Preddy received this Mustang after becoming CO of the 328th FS. His crew chief, S/Sgt Art Snyder, added the name, kill markings and a barber's pole on the right side of the nose – Snyder was also the 328th's barber. Preddy claimed four aerial victories in this Mustang, raising his total to 26.833. On Christmas Day 1944 *Cripes A'Mighty* was downed by 'friendly' flak and Maj Preddy killed.

38

P-51D-15 44-15041/*PETIE 3RD* of Lt Col John C Meyer, Deputy CO of the 352nd FG, Asch (Y-29), Belgium, December 1944

Most of the personal markings adorning this P-51D are identical to those worn by *PETIE 2ND*, except for the simplified 'Little Bastard' unit badge. Meyer scored his first aerial victories in this aircraft on 21 November 1944 when he downed three Fw 190s near Merseburg. His known kills in this fighter total 6.5, but in all probability this figure should be 11.5 – the encounter reports for his last five victories do not include the P-51's serial. 44-15041 was reassigned to Lt James Wood in February 1945.

39

P-51D-10 44-14815/*Stinky 2* of Capt William J Stangel, 328th FS, Asch (Y-29), Belgium, January 1945

Ex-bush pilot Stangel served with the RCAF and VIII Fighter Command Flight Section before joining the 328th in August 1944. He scored all five of his kills in this P-51.

40

P-51D-10 44-14237/*Moonbeam McSWINE* of Capt William T Whisner, 487th FS, Asch (Y-29), Belgium, January 1945

This aircraft was named after a character in Al Capp's comic strip *Little Abner*. 'Moonbeam' was a sexy young lady who lived with her pigs in the mythical town of 'Dogpatch'. This was Whisner's favourite P-51, and between 2 November 1944 and 1 January 1945 he enjoyed great success with it, scoring 11.5 of his 15.5 aerial kills.

41

P-51D-15 44-15041/*RICKY* of Lt James N Wood, 487th FS, Asch (Y-29), Belgium, January 1945

Lt Wood was assigned the former *PETIE 3RD* in February 1945, and he flew it in Meyer's markings for a while, although he changed the code to 'HO-Z'. He eventually renamed it *RICKY* (for his infant nephew), and painted out all but five of the swastikas from Meyer's scoreboard to reflect his own tally. Wood is officially credited with three aerial and one strafing victories – one other aerial kill that he claimed, and which was included in the group records, was never confirmed. *RICKY* was later sold to Sweden.

42

P-51D-5 44-13530/*Dutchess* of Capt Duerr Schuh, 487th FS, Chièvres (Y-84), Belgium, March 1945

Schuh joined the 487th FS in July 1944 and shot down five Bf 109s during his tour of duty. His 'big day' occurred on 26 December 1944 when he downed three Messerschmitts in the vicinity of Veldenbor. Although his encounter report does not give the aircraft markings, it is believed that he was flying *Dutchess* on this occasion.

43

P-51D-15 44-15611/*Cile VI/LUCK of the IRISH* of Capt C V Harker, 486th FS, Chièvres (Y-84), Belgium, April 1945

This was the sixth aircraft Capt Harker named for his wife Lucille, with the titling *Cile* and his *LUCK of the IRISH* artwork gracing most of his assigned aircraft starting with his P-47D in 1943. During two tours with the 486th FS Harker was credited with three strafing kills and one aircraft damaged in the air. This aircraft was later reassigned to Lt Glenn Wensch and renamed *DIABLO*.

44
P-51K-5 44-11828/*GERALDINE II* of Lt James F 'Duke' Lambright, 328th FS, Bodney, April 1945
Lambright was credited with 1.5 aerial victories, scored in his previous P-51D-10 named *Geraldine & Phylis Jean*.

45
P-51D-5 44-13806/*KENTUCKY BABE* of Lt Steve Price, 328th FS, Bodney, April 1945
Lt Price of Harlan, Kentucky, inherited Bill Hendrian's Mustang *Blondie?*, renaming it *KENTUCKY BABE*. Price destroyed one Bf 109 and damaged another during the 17 April 1945 strafing of Plattling airfield, in Germany.

46
P-51K 44-11626/*"It's SUPERMOUSE"*/Sweet Sue of Lt Robert W 'Bobby' Dodd, 328th FS, Bodney, April 1945
The idea for the name of this fighter was born after Dodd and some friends went to the movies prior to shipping out to England and saw a *Supermouse* cartoon before the feature. They immediately tagged Lt Dodd with the nickname, and it carried over to the artwork on his P-51K. Dodd flew 56 missions during his tour with the squadron, which lasted from July 1944 through to the end of the war.

47
P-51D-10 44-14696/*HELL-ER-BUST* of Capt Edwin L Heller, 486th FS, Bodney, April 1945
Capt Heller used this Mustang from November 1944 until the end of the war, and added one more aerial and seven strafing victories to his tally while flying it. At war's end his score totalled 5.5 aerial and 16.5 ground kills. Heller was the group's leading strafing ace, claiming six kills in one mission on 24 April 1944 and seven on 16 April 1945.

48
P-51D-5 44-13737/*Little Rebel* of Lt Charles C 'Buck' Pattillo, 486th FS, Bodney, April 1945
Lt Pattillo 'inherited' this Mustang from Capt Alton Wallace, who had named it *Little Rebel* (as he had done with his previous fighters). Pattillo retained the name, but personalised it by changing the colouring of the lettering from black with white outlines to white with red outlines. During his tour of duty Pattillo destroyed six aircraft (all on 16 April 1945) and damaged five others on the ground.

49
P-51D-10 44-14812/*Slender Tender & TALL* of Maj William T Halton, CO of the 487th FS, Bodney, April 1945
This was the fourth combat aircraft flown by Halton to bear the name *Slender Tender & TALL*, and it was the most successful of them all. Of his 10.5 aerial victories, Halton scored at least four of them in 44-14812, but it is possible that his total in this aircraft was as high as 9.5, for his encounter reports from Asch do not list the aircraft code or serial number. This machine was later assigned to Flt Off James White as 'HO-S' *SOCKY* and then Lt William Miller as 'HO-S' *Sweet Fern*.

50
P-51K-5 44-11556/*Sweet AND Lovely* of Lt Cuthbert A 'Bill' Pattillo, 487th FS, Bodney, April 1945
Lt Pattillo shot down an Me 262 in this aircraft on 10 April 1945. During a strafing attack six days later he added two enemy fighters to his score before being shot down by flak in this very Mustang – Pattillo spent a few days as a PoW and then returned to Bodney. This aircraft was previously assigned to Capt John Bennett, who had it marked with his standard sharksmouth nose art (and 'HO-Y' codes).

51
Noorduyn C-64A Norseman 44-70380/*JOY RIDE*, 328th FS, Bodney, Spring 1945
Aircraft such as this Norseman were used for supply flights and other official business, as well as 'booze runs'!

UNIT HERALDRY

1
21st Fighter Squadron
The emblem of the 21st Pursuit Squadron (PS) was officially approved on 20 December 1941 while the squadron was fighting for its survival during the dark days of the Japanese invasion of the Philippines. By the time the Philippines was surrendered in April 1942, the squadron had been decimated and its surviving members were reassigned. Upon the activation of the 352nd FG, the 21st PS was reformed as part of this new group, and many of the original pilots wore this patch on their flying jackets. When the squadron was redesignated as the 486th FS in May 1943, many of its members were dismayed about the loss of their heroic lineage.

2
328th Fighter Squadron
This insignia was never officially approved by the USAAF, but it was adopted nonetheless by the 328th as its unofficial crest. Its designer was Stephen Kirkel, who entitled his work 'The Spirit of Damon and Pythias – Fighter Escorting Big Friend'. It also carried the slogan 'Each would have willingly sacrificed his life for the other'.

3
486th Fighter Squadron
Like the 328th, the 486th FS's newly-designed crest was never officially approved. Nevertheless, the men of the 486th FS considered it their insignia, and it was displayed on the cover of the squadron history written at war's end.

4
487th Fighter Squadron
The 487th FS badge, designed by Sam Perry, was officially approved by the USAAF on 14 May 1943. The insignia was based on a photo of Lt Karl Waldron posing in a diaper as the 'little bastard', and carrying a machine gun as in the badge. The riding crop in his other hand is based on unit CO John Meyer's order that his pilots would carry a riding crop during the 487th's training days as a morale builder!

INDEX

References to illustrations are shown in **bold**. Plates are shown with page and caption locators in brackets.